Dare to Care

Dare to Care

Caring for our elders

Cheryl Carmichael

Illustrations by Sandra Svoboda

Dare to Care
Caring for our elders

iUniverse books may be ordered through booksellers or by contacting:

iUniverse
1663 Liberty Drive
Bloomington, IN 47403
www.iuniverse.com
1-800-Authors (1-800-288-4677)

ISBN: 978-1-4620-3146-7 (sc)

Library of Congress Control Number: 2011910098

Printed in the United States of America

iUniverse rev. date: 06/10/2011

This book is dedicated to my grandfather, Clarence, who at 94 years old was a loving caregiver to my grandmother when she turned 100 years old on December 9, 2005 in Lincoln Nebraska.

To My Readers

My mission is to keep the aging population living in their own homes.

My goal in writing *Dare to Care - Caring for our elders* is to teach new caregivers the basic concepts. This user-friendly guide to caregiving is written to adult men and women of all backgrounds. The topics are kept simple. The text is written in easy-to-follow format. Illustrations, checklists, and tables are used to help my readers.

Caregiving is a journey. That is why I chose to put a hot air balloon on the cover. The journey can be both frightening and exhilarating. Knowledgeable caregiving can reduce risk, decrease stress, and increase everyone's happiness.

Let me share my personal journey in caregiving. For over 10 years, I watched my Mother struggle with first bronchitis and then emphysema. I was both a "*long-distance*" and an "*in-town*" caregiver. For the years we lived 1200 miles apart, I spent my time on the phone. I used local resources and hired others to meet her emerging needs. After her diagnosis of emphysema, she agreed to move to my town.

Mother was an extremely independent person. She wanted to stay living in her own apartment. At first, I was able to provide supervisory care. I became her errand-runner, her chauffer, her living calendar. I evolved into her healthcare advocate and guardian. I was working full-time as her emphysema sapped her energy and her general health declined. I hired home-health aides to provide personal care - such as stand-by showers, washing her hair, and changing her linens. Twice, we hired a nurse to do home health visits during the weeks following her hospital stays and struggles with pneumonia.

I hope *Dare to Care - Caring for our elders* helps you keep your loved one living in their own homes as they age.

I wish you every success and encourage you to enjoy your journey.

Acknowledgements

Writing a book is a journey in itself. I wish to graciously thank the following individuals who have been apart of my journey. I begin with my Aunt Marie, who first introduced me to supervisory caregiving in 1986 -- instilling my vision to enable seniors to age-in-place in their home settings.

I jump years ahead thanking my wonderful teachers at Phoenix College -- especially Rose, Pat, and Mary Lynn. I appreciate my healthcare surveyors at the Arizona Department of Health -- especially Peggy, Cindy, and Sherry.

Special thanks to my dedicated proof reader Neney Sheffield and my illustrator Sandra Svoboda.

There are far too many supportive friends, prayer-partners, and family members to individually name -- but I have been continually blessed by these men and women. They have encouraged me every step of this journey. They are my angels. I lovingly thank you!

Finally I want to express my endless gratitude to my husband, Rick. He is the wind beneath my wings - enabling and supporting me through my life-journey.

Introduction

The years of 2010-2030 will have the most rapid increase in aging adults in the United States. By 2030, up to 20 percent of the population will be over 65 years old. Millions of aging adults will face retirement with limited savings. Millions will be disabled or diagnosed with chronic diseases. Millions will be diagnosed with dementia or memory loss disease. Millions will need some kind of caregiving services in their own homes.

Are you a Caregiver? Are you becoming a Caregiver?

As the baby boomer generation ages – everyday people are going to need to know as much about basic caregiving as they know about using a computer or a microwave. Do you need to learn about caregiving?

As seen on an Arizona DES Aging and Adult Administration bumper sticker:

Aging – If it's not your issue... it will be.

Developing a relationship in a new situation takes effort on the caregiver. What is your situation?

<u>As a spouse, has your role become also a caregiver to your spouse?</u> Whether gradually over the years or suddenly because of accident or illness, the job of caregiver can be new to you. Give yourself grace.

<u>Are you are suddenly caring for a parent?</u> Take the time to walk in their shoes. Give it your best effort.

<u>Have you just met?</u> If you are a volunteer or paid caregiver, take the time to get to know one another. Talk about their background, learn their cultural needs, have they lived alone, what is important to them? Build trust by sharing simple facts about yourself.

How to use this Book

Dare to Care – Caring for our elders is a basic cookbook for new or existing non-professional caregivers. It is easy-to-read. There are two major parts:

Types or levels of Caregiving

Supervisory Care, Personal Care, Memory Care, or Palliative Care

Fundamentals or building-blocks of Caregiving

Caregiving Basics, House Safety, Responding to Emergencies, Medication Services, Care Plans & Medical Records, and Gathering Financial, Planning, Legal & Documents.

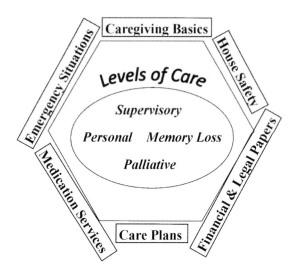

Getting Started:

Flip through the sections that present the different types of care. Determine the needs of your person. Write notes in the margins.

Review the chapters about the fundamentals of caregiving – mark useful pages and add more margin notes. Apply these techniques as your unique caregiving situation requires. Return to the book for reference, as needed.

Contents

Supervisory Care

What to look for in this section...

Physical health needs:

Hydration

Nutrition

Exercise

Functional skill needs:

Driving

Desk Work

Financial Affairs

Household Chores

Emotional health and Social well-being needs:

Activities

Getting Out

Is it a matter of money?

Keeping an Event Calendar

Senior Centers and Adult Day Health Care Centers

Supervisory care is hands-off caregiving.

Most likely you have already provided supervisory care. You provided supervisory care when you drove your person to church, took him home and cooked dinner, and then played a few games of rummy with him. Or maybe you accompanied her to the doctor's office and stayed with her during the doctor's visit, and stopped by the pharmacy on the way home to pick up the new prescription. If you like, you can add companionship, grocery shopping, laundry, house cleaning, and yard work to you list of supervisory care tasks!

Supervisory care enables a person to remain living, usually independently in their home.

What ever the task – base your actions on respect for the person receiving your care. Be kind and patient. Always promote the dignity, independence, self-determination, privacy, and choice of the individual you are helping. Be your person's advocate for their rights and needs when communicating with others.

Physical Health

Physical health caregiving addresses meeting the needs of the wellbeing of your person's body. Their body needs water or fluids, nourishment, and movement to flourish. This section discusses the importance of encouraging the drinking of fluids, the importance of providing a nutritionally balanced diet, and the importance of exercise.

Hydration

Approximately 60% of the adult body weigh is water. Water aids in the process of swallowing. Water aids in digestion and transports ingested foods. Blood is 80% water. Water is important for waste elimination. Urine is 97% water. Water helps all organ functions. Water even regulates body temperature through perspiring.

Water is more critical to survival than food.

The minimum amount of water drank should cover the total lost each day. Between 6 and 8 glasses of water or fluid is normal. The glass should hold eight-ounce or 1 cup of water. Your person's liquid intake should be sufficient to produce one quart or more of urine each day.

Determine how your person prefers to drink water -- refrigerated, with ice, room temperature, or heated. Offer water with a little lemon. Keep a glass or container of water available and visible. Using a straw might be helpful. Offer between meals.

Other beverages can be substituted occasionally as additional liquids. Other beverages do not replace the body's need for water. Beware of the caffeine in coffee or teas, the sugar in fruit juices or sodas, the salt in sports drinks, or fat content of milk. These additives in other liquids bring their own dietary issues. For instance, caffeine is a stimulant and a diuretic. As a diuretic, coffee removes water from your body.

Offer water several times each day.

Be aware of these reasons why your person might not be drinking water or other fluids.

- Is water available?

- Is your person independent and able to get water for herself?

- Is there a weakness or a disability?

- Does your person recognize the need for water?

- Is he not thirsty or have a poor appetite?

- Does she want to avoid having accidents if a bathroom is not handy?

- Does he loose sleep at night because of frequent bathroom trips?

- Be aware of any medications your person takes which act as a diuretic.

A doctor may restrict your person's fluid intake due to medical conditions such as cardiac failure, renal (kidney) failure, or pulmonary edema. It might be reasonable to limit the amount of fluids after dinner. Incontinence is discussed in *Personal Care*, but denying your person water is not the solution to incontinence.

Signs and Symptoms of Dehydration

- Look for dry tongue and skin, cracked lips, or sunken eyes.

- Does your person have a fever, nausea, dizziness, apathy, or increased confusion?

- Recent diarrhea may explain the dehydrated state.

- Constipation is common when dehydration exists.

- Is there a decrease in urinary output, is the urine concentrated, dark or smelly?

- Is your person thirsty?

Consult your doctor, if you observe frequent diarrhea, constipation, blood in urine, dark or strong smelling urine, or urgency to urinate.

Nutrition

Adequate nutrition is very important. Food and liquid nourishment supplies the body with essential nutrients. A healthy diet must include proteins, carbohydrates, limited fats, vitamins and minerals. These nutrients supply energy, grows new or repairs tissues (organs, bones, muscles, cartilage, skin, or blood), maintains and regulates the body's functions (body temperature, metabolism, digestion, constipation, or immune system).

Watch for these signs of nutritional deficiencies.

- Look for fatigue, apathy, weakness, or confusion.
- Does your person have any mouth sores?
- Has your person has a change in bowel habits - such as constipation or diarrhea?
- Can you notice recent weight loss?

There are many reasons for poor nutrition in the elderly. Disease or chronic health conditions can change the way a person eats. Mouth pain, missing or rotten teeth, or poor fitting dentures can make it hard to eat.

As a person ages, if he takes medication, these medications can cause side effects such as decreased appetite, change in taste, or drowsiness. Economic hardship plays a part in nutrition – as fresh vegetables or fruits, dairy and meat products are expensive. Can your person independently shop, buy, or cook their food.

Review the following 10 warning signs with your person. Mark any risk you determine with a check mark

Yes	Warning Sign
	I eat fewer than 2 meals per day.
	I eat alone most of the time.
	I am not always physically able to shop, cook, and/or feed myself.
	I eat few fruits or vegetables, or milk products.
	I do not always have enough money to buy the food I need.
	I have tooth or mouth problems that make it hard for me to eat.
	I have an illness or disease which has changed the kind or amount of food I eat.
	Without wanting my weight to change, I have lost or gained 10 pounds in the last 6 months.
	I have 3 or more drinks of beer, liquor, or wine almost every day.
	I take 3 or more different prescribed or over-the-counter medications each day.
	Total number of checkmarks

3-5 warning signs -- your person is at nutritional risk
6 or more signs -- your person is at high nutritional risk

Determine or seek solutions for any reason undermining your person's nutritional health.

Basic Food Groups

Food can be broken down to the following essential nutrients and functions:

- **Proteins** – contains essential amino acids which build and renews body tissues or organs
- **Carbohydrates** – provides calories for energy – this maintains the body's temperature
- **Fats** -- provides the calories for energy
- **Vitamins** -- fat soluble vs. water soluble
- **Minerals** – for examples: Iodine (thyroid), Calcium (bones, teeth, nerves), Iron (hemoglobin *red blood cells*, oxygen),
- **Water** – keeps the body hydrated

A balanced diet can be built off the basic food groups. The *Food Guide Pyramid* is now named *MyPyramid*. This USDA food guidance system is a personalized approach to healthy eating and physical activity. Recommended daily serving amounts vary – depending on your age, sex, and level of physical activity.

Create your own personalized eating plan check out <u>*www.mypyramid.gov.*</u>

The food basic groups are grains, vegetables, fruits, milk, and meat & beans.

	One-serving size	Daily recommendation	
		Men age 51+	Women age 51+
Grains – foods made from wheat, rice, oats, cornmeal, barley, or other cereal	1 ounce – ½ slice bread, 4 crackers, 1 cup cold cereal ½ cup cooked rice, pasta, or cooked cereal	6 ounce equivalents	5 ounce equivalents
Vegetables – raw or cooked; fresh, frozen, canned, or dry; whole, cut-up, or mashed	½ cup – Exception: 1 cup – raw leafy greens	5 servings	4 servings
Fruits – fresh, canned, frozen, or dried; whole, cut-up, or pureed	½ cup –	4 servings	3 servings
Milk – fluid milk, hard and soft cheeses, yogurt, ice cream or pudding;	1 cup milk, yogurt, pudding 1 ½ oz. natural cheese 2 ounces process cheese 1 ½ cups ice cream	3 servings	3 servings
Choose fat-free, low-fat, or reduced fat – *limit butter, sour cream, or cream cheese.*			
Meat & Beans – protein foods; meat, poultry, fish, dry beans or peas, eggs, nuts, and seeds; lean or low-fat.	1 ounce – cooked meat, fish, or poultry, ¼ cup dry (before cooked) beans or peas, ¼ c baked or refried beans, 2 ounces of tofu, 1 egg, ½ ounce of nuts or seeds, 1 Tablespoon peanut butter	5 ½ ounce equivalents	5 ounce equivalents

Making Good Nutritional Choices

Whole grain foods contain the entire grain kernel and refined grain foods have been milled. It is recommended that at least ½ of all the grains eaten should be whole grains. Look for the labels which advertize *whole grains*. The dietary fiber from whole grains helps reduce cholesterol and may lower the risk of heart disease. Fiber in your diet also helps reduce diverticulitis and constipation.

Get into the habit of reading package labels.

Calcium is a mineral the body needs to stay healthy. It is important for strong bones and teeth. Calcium helps prevent some chronic diseases – such as osteoporosis, hypertension, heart disease, and colon cancer. Older adults need three or four servings a day from the milk group (or soybeans and other soy products) to meet their calcium needs.

Talk with your doctor if you think you are lactose intolerant. Many people can drink at least a cup of milk with a meal without any problems. Eat more cheese, as most of the lactose is removed when the milk is made into cheese. Yogurt contains *friendly bacteria* that helps digest lactose easily.

Omega-3 fatty acids found in oils are good for your heart and brain. Yet, oils and fats are high in calories. Use **fats and oils** sparingly. Foods that contain fats or oils are butter, margarine, mayonnaise, certain salad dressings, and cooking oils. Nuts, olives, some fish, and avocados also are naturally high in oils. Whole milk has more than three times the saturated fat than low-fat (1%) milk. The daily allowance of fats and oils for older adults is 5-6 teaspoons.

Be sensible about **salt**. Table salt contains **sodium**. The body uses sodium to maintain blood volume, regulate water balance, transmit nerve impulses, and perform other vital functions. But sodium is also one factor that is associated with high blood pressure. One teaspoon of salt has 2400mg of sodium. The daily allowance for adults is 1,100-2,400mg of sodium. Ask your doctor or dietitian what sodium level is safe you your person.

A few dietary habits can reduce sodium without greatly changing the diet. Choose fresh fruits, vegetables, and meats. Processed foods such as soups, frozen or canned foods, and packaged foods usually have salt added. Look for product labels that say low-sodium. Use lemon, pepper, herbs, spices, finely chopped garlic or onion, or horseradish to flavor the food in place of salt. Go easy on condiments such as ketchup, mustard, salad dressings, soy sauce, relish, pickles, and olives – these all contain sodium. Leave the salt shaker off the table.

Enjoy sweets in moderation. Limit foods and beverages with added **sugar**. Added sugar is just that – added sugar. Most processed or prepared foods contain added sugar. Examples of foods that contain added sugars are regular soft drinks, candy, most desserts (unless labeled sugar-free), fruit drinks, and bakery items. Look for added sugars on the food labels – sugar, sucrose, corn syrup, fructose, etc.

Avoid products when the ingredients begin with *high fructose corn syrup*. Being high in calories, this form of sugar can increase weight gain increasing your person's risks of obesity, diabetes, elevated cholesterol, or liver damage. It is also linked to an increased risk of hypertension.

Some forms of alcohol are higher in sugar content like beer and after dinner liqueurs. Check with your person's doctor if a glass of wine can be enjoyed with your evening meal.

Therapeutic diets

If your doctor places your person on a specific therapeutic diet, purchase a diet manual that teaches you about the diet and provides you with a list of acceptable foods and menus. Refer to the USDA M*yPyramid.gov* web site. Meet with a Registered Dietitian to discuss your questions and concerns.

The following table shows many therapeutic diets.

Diet	Description
Clear Liquid	Gives the GI tract a rest. Clear juices, broth, popsicles, gelatin, and teas
Full Liquid	Includes clear liquids and adds milk, yogurt, pudding, and smooth cream soups
Soft or pureed	Foods that can be eaten with a spoon – no chewing required. Use food processor.
Low-fat, Low-cholesterol	The Cardiac diet. Foods low in saturated fat, cholesterol, and salt. Whole grains, abundant vegetables and fruit, lean meat, poultry, and fish are emphasized
Diabetic	Keeps blood glucose levels under control. Low in sugar and fat.
Low Sodium	Avoid processed foods. Keep sodium intake at 1,100 – 1,500 mg per day
Bland	Ulcers and GI issues. Avoid spicy foods and limit sodium.
Food Allergy	Nuts, shell-fish, fish, MSG, aged/molded cheeses (blue, parmesan), seeds – any others.

Weight gain or weight loss

There are special considerations for the elderly relating to weight changes. Older bodies require fewer calories. The body functions or metabolism are slower and usually the person is less active. Weight gain can be the result of diabetes or other chronic illnesses, from reduced exercise, or by eating too many calories. The estimated daily calorie need for the elderly person is noted in the next table.

Calorie need		Moderate physical activity *most days*
Men – age 51+	**Women – age 51+**	
2000 calories	1600 calories	Less than 30 minutes
2200 calories	1800 calories	More than 30 minutes
2800 calories	2200 calories	More than 60 minutes

The elderly experience a decreased sense of taste and smell. Think of eating a meal you can't smell or taste – it reduces your desire to eat. In the digestive system there is a decrease in the absorption of nutrients. Medications may also interfere with absorption of nutrients. To fight weight loss, there is a need for increased balances of protein, calcium, and B12. Additional high-protein beverages or shakes can add calories at meals or as snacks.

Unintended or sudden weight loss is an immediate health concern. Nutritional deficiencies and the warning signs presented at the beginning of this section may be reasons for weight loss. Call your doctor to report unexplained or sudden weight loss.

Seek nutritional advice from a Registered Dietitian if your person is over or under weight.

Obesity,

Obesity among the elderly is a growing health-related concern. Many of these obese elderly were obese middle-aged adults. This excess body weight in the middle-aged adult can contribute to chronic diseases such as hypertension, diabetes mellitus, cardiovascular disease, and osteoarthritis as the person ages. Obesity in the elderly can lead to physical impairment, reduced activity levels, and increased dependence on others. Depression is common with the obese elderly.

Seek your doctor's help with a weight loss plan, which balances diet and exercise and also addresses the physical, medical, and caregiving needs if your person is diagnosed with obesity.

3 Meals and 2 Snacks

Breakfast	Lunch	Dinner	2 Snacks
Cold cereal fat-free milk Small banana Slice toast	Tuna (2 ounce) sandwich with lettuce Raw vegetables Fruit cup 1 cup fat-free milk	Chicken (3 ounce) breast Small potato Dinner salad Whole wheat roll 1 cup low-fat Ice Cream	Morning: Apple slices Afternoon: Oatmeal cookie
grain, milk, fruit, grain	protein, grain, fruit, vegetables x 2, milk	Protein, vegetables x 2, grain, milk	fruit, grain

Plan one week of meals and snacks to serve with regard to your person's nutritional needs. Base your menus on their food preferences, eating habits, health conditions, and customs. Offer a variety of foods. Split the daily recommended servings between three meals – breakfast, lunch, and dinner – and two snacks. The following example menu is based on a woman's needs. The serving sizes would be slightly larger for a man.

Creating Menus and Grocery Lists for shopping is covered in Chapter 1.

Enjoying meal time

Eating is a social activity. Eating provides the opportunity for social interaction, it is a time for pleasure, improves nutrition, and is an opportunity to enhance dignity. Creating a pleasant and inviting meal time increases your person's willingness to eat.

Serve the meal at a dining table in a bright room. Turn off the television. Silence the phone. Turn on the soft music. Plan to eat together and engage in a conversation throughout the entire meal.

Involve everyone by asking your person to help set the table with the placemats, napkins, and silverware. Have them enjoying a beverage, munching on a couple of crackers, or starting on their salad while you finish preparing the meal. Name or describe all the foods and encourage positive responses.

Exercise

Physical activity or exercise causes blood and fluids to move through joints, providing nourishment and removing wastes. Exercise is good for your bones – it helps maintain or improve joint flexibility, range of motion, and bone health. It improves balance -- reducing the risk of falls. Exercise is helpful for stress relief.

There are three major types of exercise.

Aerobic exercise such as walking is beneficial because the movement encourages blood to flow through hip, leg and foot joints. It also promotes cardiovascular health and weight control.

Resistance or strength training is practiced using weight machines, free weights or even soup cans or old milk jugs filled with water. Strength training creates stronger muscles and stronger bones. In your legs these muscles help to protect and stabilize the joint and helps absorb shock. Improving the strength in the thigh muscles, helps improve mobility.

Flexibility or stretching exercises should be done on daily. Moving joints through their entire range of motion keeps them from stiffening and causing pain.

Determine how much and what type of exercise your person has been doing. Some amount of exercise a day is good. Build up gradually setting a goal of exercising a total of 30 minutes per day most days of the week. Exercising three separate 10 minute sessions can be as beneficial as one 30 minute session.

> ***Ask your doctor for guidance in developing a physical activity program that is right for your person.***

For those who have arthritis or joint disorders, it might be more comfortable to exercise in warm-water pool. Water eases muscle movement and supports tender joints.

Functional Skill Limitations

For supervisory care *functional skills* are defined as your person's ability to perform the tasks required by your person to live independently. Slower reflexes, decreasing vision, decreasing hearing, pain, frailness, lack of energy, or decreasing physical strength are all examples of functional skill limitations. Perhaps your person is simply not physically, emotionally or cognitively able to keep doing tasks they have always performed. This section discusses topics where you can meet your person's changing needs to overcome their limitations.

Driving

When a person can not safely drive, they give up a portion of their independence. How are they to do their shopping – go out to eat – get to church – or even get to their medical appointments?

Put your heads together and determine how you can provide adequate transportation. Is there a neighbor or friend that can take your person shopping for groceries when they go? Some grocery stores offer on-line orders and home delivery. Ask a church member to provide transportation to/from church services or evening church meetings. Determine a specific person to run necessary errands and stay for a visit on a weekly basis. Consider a lunch or dinner date every Thursday. Create a list of family and friends who have offered to provide rides.

Explore public transportation. Can you arrange for a cab or senior community-based door-to-door wheelchair accessible van or bus to take your person to and from medical appointments? Does the local senior center offer transportation to/from the senior center?

Desk Work

Does your person remember to keep their medical appointment? Is she frustrated with phone-tree options when she makes a call? Does his hand hurt when he writes? Are the bills being paid?

Desk work tasks can be shared – again put your heads together to determine the need and the solution.

Helpful suggestions:

- Create a desk or wall calendar. Have space to write appointments, outings, or visits.
- Label a tablet where your person can write down questions or requests of help for you when you come to visit or call.
- Offer to handle calls about insurance or medical questions or call together using a speaker phone.
- Offer to type as they dictate their holiday or birthday letters. Address, stamp, and mail cards or letters.
- Create a list of address labels for holiday letters. Provide return address labels.
- Set up the computer for easy access to the internet.. Set up a printer.
- Set up an e-mail account.
- Together take a computer introduction class at the local Senior Center.

Financial Affairs

Discuss your person's ability to continuing to handle their own financial affairs. This topic like driving might require your person to give up another portion of their independence. The consequences of unpaid bills can be costly in account charges and even service stoppages – like turning off the electric power.

Determine if your person wants to keep control of the checkbook, share control, or prefers to turn over the entire process to a trusted family member.

<u>Easing the effort:</u>

- Set up a process for your person to follow.
  - o Determine a drawer or basket for the checkbook, pens, stamps, and envelops.
  - o Create a bill paying folder.
  - o Create a filing system for insurance or medical statements, paid bills, tax documents, and investment statements.
  - o Purchase a paper shredder.
- Set up direct deposit of income sources – social security, pensions, or annuity payments.
- Set up automated payments for regular monthly bills like mortgage or rent, utilities, or charity pledges.
- Set up on-line bill payment using your person's checking account for various bills like credit card, insurance, or
- Rent a safety deposit box at a local bank for important financial and legal documents.

Sharing the load:

- You can get together every two weeks and pay the bills together.
- As a bookkeeper, you can do everything to get the bill ready to mail – including filling out the check, completing the insert for the bill, addressing and stamping the envelope. Your person can review the bill and sign their name on the check to approve payment.
- Review and balance the monthly checking statement.
- Review and discuss monthly or quarterly savings/investment statements.
- Compare insurance payments with actual medical bills. Filing reviewed documents.

Responsible fiduciary money management:

- If your person voluntarily asks you to handle their financial matters you can arrange for the bills to your home address.
- Your name and/or ability to sign checks can be added to your person's checking account with your person's written approval on a bank form.
- As above, set up direct deposit of income sources, automated payments, and on-line bill payments.
- Keep separate accounts – theirs in their name and your own personal accounts.
- Consider a Durable Power of Attorney – see *Advanced Directives* in Chapter 6.
- Consider consulting with a financial planner or accountant for more complicated financial matters.
- Keep statements, paid bills, documents in a safe and separate filing system from your own.

Household Chores

Home repair, yard work, and household cleanliness often include tasks requiring physical effort. When these tasks are needed or left undone your person's safety and well-being can be compromised.

Does ceiling light bulb that needs replacement in the kitchen require a ladder to change it? Does the lawn need mowing every week in the summer? Are there piles of newspapers, magazines, and junk mail on every surface in the living room? Does the kitchen smell of stale garbage? Are there dirty dishes on the counter or dirty laundry piled in the bedroom? This list can be endless.

> ### *Review (Chapter 2) The House They Live In for home repair, yard work, and inside safety.*

Discuss your observations and concerns with your person. Once again, determine what help or services meet the needs of your person. Providing help in these areas frees up your person to spend their energy in areas of relaxation, socialization, and activities of daily living.

The following table lists different workers, types of service, and frequency of services provided. Included in the list of services are other areas of supervisory care services discussed within this section. You might consider hiring some of these tasks to be done. You can also use this table to create your own table of family or friends who might volunteer to provide the services on a regular basis. If your person is living independently – leave a completed copy on their refrigerator – as a reminder of scheduled help.

Who	What	When
Family, friend, church member, neighbor Paid senior van or bus Taxi	Transportation Dial-A-Ride, Red Cross, Senior Center Local phone book	√ scheduled as needed √ routinely as needed
Chore workers	Yard work, snow removal, windows	√ as needed
Handyman	Home repairs, ramps or grab bars	√ as needed
Housekeeper	Cleans bathroom, kitchen, straightens, dusts, vacuums, mops floors, changes linens, does laundry, removes trash, other tasks as requested	√ monthly √ weekly
Homemaker	Light housework, shops, does laundry, prepares meals, waters plants	√ weekly √ daily
Companion	Shops, prepares meals, desk work tasks, visits, plays table games, reads out-loud	√ weekly √ daily
Brian – grandson	*Mows grass, sweeps patio, takes trash barrel to street*	√ *Thursdays - summer*

Emotional Health and Social Well-being

Psychosocial health is defined as a person's mental, cognitive, emotional and social well-being. Emotional health is how a person thinks about themselves and reacts to their current situations. Social well-being is how a person interacts with others.

The topics discussed in this section can be applied to *all individuals* – including the caregiver who is living with or caring for their person. Keys to emotional health and social well-being are being involved in meaningful activities, positive mental attitudes, looking forward to tomorrow, meaningful relationships, and spirituality.

> *Memory Loss Care discusses caring for your person with a mental or cognitive diagnosis.*

Activities

Studies have shown as a person ages – those who stay actively engaged – live longer and live better lives. Activities can be broken down into social, recreational, and habilitative. It is important to determine and focus on your person's preferences about activities. One size does not fit all. Every day needs to include some form of activity.

Social

Social activities include interactions with others. They can include activities with others in the home, in the family, in the neighborhood. Church activities such as worship meetings, bible studies, or ladies mission groups are social activities. Outside support systems would include special interest groups such as a Parkinson's support group, a bridge club meeting, or meeting to play billiards or horseshoes at your community center.

Recreational

Recreational activities focus on enjoyment, amusement, entertainment, relaxation, and/or play. They include forms of exercise – walking, swimming, golfing, hiking, or dancing to music. Going to a movie or shopping at the mall is recreational. Playing cards, table games, or dominos is recreational. Reading a book or listening to music can bring your person relaxation. Pursing new or old hobbies, such as knitting, working crossword puzzles, woodworking or gardening brings enjoyment.

Habilitative

Habilitative activities focus on the purpose of enhancing the emotional well-being or preventing the regression of intellect or functional skills of your person. These activities are along the same line as rehabilitative activities which focus on restoring physical, psychosocial, and functional losses. Walking around the block might serve as a habilitative activity – if as a caregiver you require some personal time for just your thoughts and enjoyment. The same walk with your person who has recently completed his physical therapy for a hip replacement would be a rehabilitative activity.

Playing a game of bingo serves as an example of how an activity can be social, recreational, and habilitative. Others play with you. You have fun trying to win the game. You keep your mind active checking the card after each number is called.

Getting Out

What are the reasons your person is unable or unwilling to leave the house and be active with their local communities?

- Does your person live alone?
- Is your aunt staying home because she is afraid to drive?
- Is your mother caring for your father in their home?
- Are you caring for your person in your home?

Discuss the needs of your person, seeking solutions that free them to think of themselves. Everyone needs a change of scene on a regular basis.

- Is encouragement all they need?
- Do they need transportation or companionship to get out?
- Do they need a back-up caregiver or companion – so that they can leave their person at home and not worry?
- Do you need a back-up caregiver?

After you find a solution – look to what they or you want to do with this new-found freedom.

Consider these activities:

- Volunteer - volunteer work is reciprocal – you give something and you get something back.
- Plan an enjoyable outing with others – go window shopping, eat lunch out, or see a movie.
- Take or teach a class – interaction with other students stimulates your mind.
- Join a support group, find a golfing partner, join a bible study, or even get to the gym.
- Plan a trip or ask other family or friends to come visit you.

Is it a matter of money?

Statistics for number of elderly living on incomes at or below poverty level are only getting worse since the depression of 2009. While sitting on a patio chair – watching the humming birds feed on the honeysuckle vine on a sunny morning doesn't cost a dime – it is not free to learn how to paint that picture using water colors. There is the cost of the class given by a local artist, the cost of the painting supplies, and maybe the cost of getting to the class.

If your person does not have financial independence focus on keeping the costs low or free when planning activities. Discuss options with other family members who do have the means to share their resources. If your person wants to visit family far away, consider buying the airplane ticket early to save money and giving it as a birthday or holiday gift. Charity can begin at home – or at least within the family unit.

Look for free or low-cost events. Watch the local paper for classes, music in the parks, social groups, support groups, free days at the zoo or museum. Attend a holiday celebration or festival on the weekend. Find schedules for local high school or college ballgames, music programs, or theater events.

Keep an Event Calendar

Calendars communicate future events and preserve a history of past events. When your person lives independently alone keeping an event calendar can be a reminder and a journal of daily activities. If there are multiple caregivers involved a calendar can be a communication tool.

What gets scheduled on the event calendar:

- Community events – dances at the senior center, free day at the zoo, bible study at the church
- Family events – birthday dinner at Joe's, BBQ at Joe's, Jill's school play, Judy's visit from Colorado
- Doctor appointments, lab work, blood pressure checks, dental appointments
- Hair appointments, dog grooming, organ lesson, golf tee times
- Dates the housekeeper comes, grocery shopping with the neighbor, volunteer days

What is noted on the event calendar:

- Who called or dropped by to visit
- When and how much exercise was done – walked w/ Joe 30 minutes
- Did grocery shopping, paid bills, sent get-well card
- Yard was mowed, trees trimmed, snow shoveled off walkways

Keep the calendar in a specific place – easy to access or read.

Purchase a calendar that lays flat or hangs on a hook with large daily boxes. Keep a pen available for jotting in entries. Save the calendars for reference.

Activity Calendars

The prior *Exercise* and *Activity* sections discuss the need for some type of exercise most days and the importance of being actively engaged in social, recreational, and functional activities on a regular basis.

A personalized activity calendar can be created to encourage your person to be active everyday. Schedule their activities – like meetings for a retired worker or task-lists for the woman who raised three children.

Senior Centers and Adult Day Health Care Centers

Senior Centers are located in many neighborhoods for convenient access. These centers provide an array of activities and programs for older adults, such as – meals, community outings, special entertainment, education, and social activities or events.

Adult Day Health Care Centers are licensed centers which provide daytime care and assistance to seniors with disabilities who cannot stay at home alone. They offer a wide variety of social, recreational, medical, and therapeutic services in a supportive environment. They offer a stimulating setting in which your person can renew their self-worth, regain skills required for daily living, and have fun with others!

For a caregiver – an Adult Day Health Care Center offers welcome relief, support, and peace of mind. Consider enrolling your person 2-3 days a week to give yourself time for activities, errands, or even a quite day at home alone.

> *Senior Centers and Adult Day Health Care Centers*
> *provide monthly activity or program calendars.*

They show what is happening on the days the centers are open. Post these calendars if your person attends so they can look forward to going to the center to participate in the activities.

Personal Care

What to look for in this section...

Functional Skills

Activities of Daily Living:

Grooming

Dressing

Eating

Mobility and Transfer

Toileting

Bathing

Medication Services

Vital Signs:

Body Temperatures

Respiration

Pulse, Blood Pressure

Weight

Routine Personal Care Topics:

Infection Control – Washing Hands

Skin Care

Non-ambulatory Personal Care

Personal care is defined as hands-on caregiving or care that requires the caregiver to physically touch the person.

Personal care is required when the person you are caring for needs help with common *Activities of Daily Living* or ADL(s). A simple example of personal care starts when your room-mate in college broke her arm playing soccer. Every morning you helped her put on a clean shirt and buttoned her buttons. You might have buttoned her jeans and buckled her belt. If she also broke her ankle – you might have pushed her around in a wheelchair.

Personal care includes taking a person's temperature, blood pressure, or giving them a neck and shoulder rub. Personal care moves into the boundaries of your person's independence. You are working in their physical space. Remember, what ever the task – base your actions on respect for the person receiving your care. Be kind and patient.

Allow your person to be as self-reliant as possible, even if they go slow or are not as skilled as they once used to be. Always promote the dignity, independence, self-determination, privacy, and choice of this individual.

Review "Communication" in Basic Caregiving (Chapter 1).

Functional Skills

Physical health is defined as the wellbeing of a person's body. The table below shows a short list of examples that might present the person with limited physical health.

Diagnosis	Person's body	Limits functional skills
Stroke	Partial paralysis of left side	Person can't use left hand, arm, leg, or foot.
Emphysema	Breathing is impaired: reduces oxygen to all parts of the body	Slows all movements of body, fatigue, trouble standing alone
Hip or Knee replacement	Requires rehabilitative therapy to restore the use of the joint.	Limits use of healing leg

Psychosocial health is defined as the mental, cognitive, emotional, and social well being of a person. Common diagnoses might include depression, traumatic brain injury (TBI), Parkinson's disease, or Alzheimer's disease. For example, a person with memory loss might be physically able to brush his own teeth, but the caregiver must remind him to brush his teeth after meals.

Depending upon your person's physical or psychosocial health needs, the personal care you provide varies. Understanding their diagnosis enables you to assess your person's functional skills. Functional skills are defined as the person's ability to perform activities of daily living.

Consider these three different levels of help. Remind the person to shower. Start and set the shower water to a safe temperature and stay in the bathroom while the person showers. Or actually give the person the shower with the aid of a shower chair and shower hose.

"Functional Assessment" is found in Care Plans (Chapter 5).

Activities of Daily Living

Grooming

Begin and end each day with the washing of the person's face and hands. Offer a warm washcloth and encourage the person to be as independent as possible with this task. Washing and drying the skin is refreshing, relaxing, and promotes a person's self-esteem.

Brushing or combing hair increases scalp circulation and stimulates oil glands to lubricate scalp and hair. If help is needed, bush or comb the hair in all sections from the scalp to the ends. Finish by styling hair around face and neck.

Oral hygiene encourages appetite by removing bad tastes from the mouth and prevents dental problems. Oral hygiene includes flossing, brushing teeth, gums, and tongue, and denture care. Encourage or provide oral hygiene two or three times each day. Notify your dentist if you detect any abnormal dental or denture conditions.

Shaving promotes self-esteem and most men have shaved every morning before going to work. Continue this routine. Provide an electric razor. Offer help when needed.

Other daily grooming tasks might include using deodorant, applying lotion to the skin, putting on rouge or lipstick or using lip balm.

Place dentures, hearing aids, or glasses in their storage containers in the same location when they are not in use.

Fingernail, foot, and toenail care helps to prevent infection or injury. Every day, observe the hands and feet for any redness, cracks, bruises, and corns.

If you need to trim nails, begin with soaking the hands or feet in warm water. Wash, clean, and completely dry them. Using nail clippers trim nails, and then file sharp edges off with an emery board. Lotion can be applied to hands and tops and bottoms of feet. To stimulate circulation or bring relaxation, end the nail care with a gentle massage to each hand or foot.

> *If your person is diagnosed with Diabetes, consult with your doctor before cutting fingernails or toenails.*

Dressing

Getting dressed promotes self-esteem. Choosing what to wear provides opportunities for decision making.

Offer choice – button-down or pull-over shirt – blue or red; dress, skirt, pants, or shorts – flowered or solid; slip-ons or tennis shoes. Ask if they want a sweater, vest, or scarf. What about their well-worn watch or colored beads?

Looser, stretchy clothes are easier to put on, consider using pants with elastic waists. Buy similar looking items, if favorites are always chosen. Buy comfortable underwear; substituting boxers for briefs or a cotton t-shirt for a bra. Shoes must be as functional as they are comfortable. Offer only non-skid shoes or slippers. Consider shoes with Velcro straps.

Layout items in order used to dress. Encourage independence, offering assistance when needed.

If you assist with dressing – socks or knee-hi(s), pant legs, or sleeves should be gathered before putting them on. For a looser top, put the arms in first and then pull over the head. Remove in reverse order.

If your person has weakness or paralysis on one side, put clothing on the weak side first, then the strong side. Support the weak or paralyzed side at all times. To remove clothing start with the strong side first and then finish with the weak side. Observe skin integrity.

Finish your dressing care with a complement or praise.

Mobility and Transfer

A person is **ambulatory**, if they walk – with or without assistance. A person can walk with assistance by using a cane, a walker, a hallway railing, or by holding on to a caregiver's arm. This added assistance increases the person's balance and helps to reduce falls.

A person is **mobile** if they move about independently with the assistance of a wheelchair or electric scooter, even with some assistance.

When a person is not capable walking without the assistance of another person or cannot independently move their body from a wheelchair to a bed, chair, or toilet, the person is described as **non-ambulatory**.

> *Before you assist your person – plan and discuss what you are planning on doing.*

If your person is frail, you might need to guide them to safely stand up. While they are still lying on their bed, tell them that you want them to swing their legs toward you and sit up on the bed. You can put slippers on their feet. Place their walker in front of them. Tell them to place their hands on the arms of the walker and then tell them to use their legs to stand up. Let them find their standing balance before asking them to walk.

It is important for you as a caregiver to learn and practice good body mechanics when you assist your person with walking or help them with moving from one place to another. Use good posture. Keep your body aligned properly, with your back straight, knees bent, and weight evenly balanced on both feet. Encourage the person to use their own body and strength.

> *Lock the wheelchair wheels stationary before transfer of person.*

If your person lacks balance, encourage your person to use a cane or walker. Check with your doctor or home health nurse to investigate what canes, walkers, electric scooters, or wheelchairs might best meet the need to keep your person as independent as possible.

Eating

As discussed in *Supervisory Care*, adequate nutrition is very important. Making mealtime a social and pleasurable event encourages your person to eat. Set an attractive table. Eat with your person whenever possible. Do not rush the meal. It can take up to an hour to enjoy the entire meal. Attend to toileting prior to beginning the meal.

Serve the meal at a dining table in a bright room. Use straight back chairs. Encourage your person to sit in an upright position with his feet flat on the floor. His head is slightly forward and about 12 inches from the food.

If your person uses a wheelchair, it might better to transfer them to a chair for hip support, when possible. The chair might be taller and can usually be pushed closer to the table. If your person has poor sitting balance, place her forearms on the table to help stabilize her body.

Encourage as much independence with eating as possible. Make the most of your person's abilities. Use a bowl or a deep dish instead of a plate, with a spoon instead of a fork. Use spoons with large handles. Use light weight cups with large handles or mugs with lids to prevent spilling. Fill the glass half full and use straws that bend.

When you serve the meal, check the food temperature.

Prepare meals that are appropriate for your person. Serve foods as your person requires it to be prepared, such as cut-up or chopped. For ground, soft, or pureed foods consider using a 3-section divided plate to separate foods. As you serve the meal, name each food. If your person is blind, use the clock method to identify the placement on the plate.

If your person has difficulty holding a fork or spoon try serving finger foods like cut up chicken, French fries, cut green beans, and pealed cucumber slices. Serve a sandwich. Allow your person to eat with their hands. Give your person plenty of time to eat.

Do not criticize your person's eating habits.

If your person needs assistance with eating to regain eating skills start with verbal cues or instructions like *"pick up your spoon; put some potatoes on it; put the spoon in your mouth"*. You can gently place your person's hand on or near the spoon. You can point to the potatoes on the plate. Speak slowly. Be clear and repeat instructions with the same words each time.

You can also use the <u>watch me</u> technique. For example, hold a spoon and showing the person how to eat from the bowl. Be patient. Do not encourage him to eat faster.

You can use the <u>hand-over-hand</u> technique by putting a spoon or fork in your person's hand, placing your hand around theirs, and then lifting both your hands to the person's mouth for a bite. Let your person feed herself as much as she can – providing too much assistance makes them less able to help themselves.

When you need to feed your person, first identify the food on the plate. If in doubt, test the temperature of any food item, by placing a small amount on the inside of your wrist. Wipe off your wrist with a napkin or paper towel. Use a teaspoon and fill it half full for each bite. Place the food in the center of their tongue. Allow time to chew and swallow. Alternate the solid food with a sip of fluid. Do not force your person to eat food they do not want to eat.

Be alert for signs of choking.

If your person has trouble swallowing, avoid foods that are difficult to chew thoroughly or that can get caught in the throat, such as raw carrots. Using abdominal thrusts to clear the airway are discussed in Chapter 3 under *Choking.*

Toileting

Incontinence is not the normal outcome of aging. The loss of bladder or bowel control can be caused by many reasons – an acute illness, a chronic illness, various foods or beverages, medications, or forgetfulness. Because incontinence is distressing, it is important to deal with it. Seek medical treatment – your doctor can determine the cause and offer ways to help.

Consult your doctor, if you observe diarrhea, constipation, blood in urine, dark or strong smelling urine, unexpected leakage of urine, or the urgency to urinate.

Incontinence is embarrassing to anyone. Be considerate and maintain a casual attitude. Offer as much privacy as possible. There are a number of incontinence products available. Check with your medical supply company or local pharmacy to determine the best adult incontinence and personal hygiene product for your person's needs.

Show respect – use the words underwear or pad – never diaper.

If your incontinent person is able, encourage them to be as independent as possible with using the bathroom. Try reminding the person to use the bathroom every two hours. Establish a routine daily schedule to encourage bowel movements.

Have incontinent supplies handy. Place a covered trash can with plastic bags in bathroom. Install grab bars by the toilet or a raised toilet seat to make the task safer. Use good body mechanics if you help the person sit down or stand up from the toilet. Give them privacy. Hang a ingle-bell on the wall above the toilet. When it is not safe to leave the bathroom, look away or turn your back on your person.

If an accident occurs and you are needed to help change the wet or soiled underwear, ask your person to tell you as soon as possible. Unattended incontinence can lead to skin infection. When your person needs your help with wiping or cleansing follow the steps for Perineal Care.

Step-by-Step – Perineal Care

Using wipes or a soft washcloth and warm water remove urine or bowel movement and cleanse area. Wipe front to back (labia to rectum, female) and (scrotum to rectum, male).

Providing perineal care to a person in a bed –

Female: Remove adult hygiene undergarment. Remove excess urine or bowel movement with a wipe before washing the area. Begin with the outer labia and then the inner labia. Separate the inner labia and wash. Wash the entire pubic area, rectum, and between the legs. Use downward (front to back) strokes.

Male: Begin at the end of the penis, retracting uncircumcised skin if needed, washing down the shaft of the penis. Wash under the scrotum and then the rectal area using front to back strokes.

Both: Use a new side of washcloth for every stroke, rinsing washcloth as needed. Rinse entire area to remove soap residue. Dry entire area. Observe skin integrity. Apply a moisture-barrier creams or powder. Put on a clean undergarment.

See Palliative Care for complete Bed Bathing Guidelines

At night, use night lights in the bedroom and bathrooms. Make sure the pathway is clear to avoid falls. Put a bell by the bed, if the person requires help to the bathroom. Consider using a bed-side commode. Have your person use absorbent underwear and put washable pads on top of the bottom sheet.

If the person you are caring for has a colostomy appliance or a bladder catheter consult with your doctor, home health nurse, or physical therapist to train you in the proper technique to empty or change these bags.

Both you and your person should wash your hands after any bathroom visit.

Bathing

Bathing cleanses the skin removing odors, dirt, and perspiration from the body. It is an opportunity to assess skin integrity. It stimulates circulation, provides moderate exercise, refreshes and relaxes.

If bathing is uncomfortable to your person – if they refuse, resist, or are a physical challenge or risk for you to handle – then consider hiring a home health aide 2 to 3 times a week to help with bathing.

Create a private atmosphere in a warm bath room with no drafts. Promote independence and encourage self-care during bathing. Begin by gathering the towels, wash cloth, soap, and shampoo. Lay out clean clothes or a bathrobe.

Bathing Guidelines

- **Turn the cold water on first. Turn the cold water off last. Avoid scalds.**

- For tub baths –

  fill the tub half full – circulate and test the water with the inside of your wrist.

- For a shower the water should be warm not hot –

  test the water with the inside of your wrist.

- **The water temperature should not be above 105°F.**

- Ask if the water temperature is comfortable to your person, <u>before</u> they get in the bath or shower.

- Use a shower chair and shower hose.

- Assist, as needed, by helping your person into the tub or shower, in washing, rinsing, and drying.

Medication Services

The caregiver becomes involved with providing medication services, when the person requires assistance in the self-administration of medication or actual medication administration.

Providing medication assistance to a person taking medication might include:

♦ Setting up the medication organizer

♦ Reminding the person that it is time to take a medication

♦ Opening the medication container

♦ Pouring or placing the specified dosage into a container or into the resident's hand

♦ Creating or completing the medication log sheet

Medication administration means the application of medication to its ultimate destination on the body of the person. Medication administration might include:

♦ Placing a pill in the person's mouth

♦ Injecting insulin into your person's leg or body

♦ Placing a suppository into their rectum

Medication Services (Chapter 4) expands on medication topics and providing assistance with medications

Blood Sugar

Diabetes is a chronic disease. The two main types of diabetes are insulin-dependent (type 1) and non-insulin-dependent (type 2). Type 1 requires oral medication or injections of insulin to control the blood glucose (also called blood sugar). Type 2 is frequently managed by diet, exercise, and weight management. The normal range of blood sugar varies during the day as shown below.

Most often type 2 diabetes is found in elderly persons. The aging body looses the ability to use carbohydrates, proteins, and fats effectively. There is a decrease in glucose or sugar tolerance.

Hypoglycemia is low blood sugar below 70. It can be caused by too little food, extra exercise, too much insulin or diabetes medication. The onset of symptoms is sudden and may progress to insulin shock.

Hyperglycemia is high blood sugar above 200. It can be caused by too much food, too little insulin, stress or an illness. The onset of symptoms is gradual and may progress to a diabetic coma.

If your person is diagnosed with diabetes, the person and/or caregiver needs special training by a diabetes educator, nurse, or registered dietitian to learn how to test blood sugar and control the blood sugar.

Monitoring Blood Sugar

Checking blood sugar can be done at home – using a blood glucose meter – as often as directed by a health care provider. The self-check tells you what your person's blood sugar is at the time of the test. Self-checks help you see how food, physical activity, and diabetes medication affects their blood sugar. Self-checks are usually done before meals and/or at bedtime. The readings from self-checks help you manage your person's diabetes day by day – or even hour by hour.

Some glucose meters keep records of readings electronically. If not, keep a written record of the self-check results in your person's care plan. Record their targets and the date, time, and results. Review the readings with their health care provider. Discuss and document specific goals for your person's blood sugar levels during their doctor visits.

Below is a sample Blood Sugar Self Check record:

Name:		**Blood Sugar Checks**
Before meals:	**1-2 hours after meals**	**Bedtime**
Usual goal 90 to 130	Usual goal below 180	Usual goal is 110 to 150
6/12 4pm 124		*6/12 9:30pm 135*

Oxygen Therapy

Oxygen therapy is used generally to relieve hypoxia – a condition in which the body is not receiving adequate oxygen due to an insufficiency of oxygen in the blood. Common illnesses which require oxygen therapy include pneumonia, chronic bronchitis, and other chronic obstructive pulmonary diseases (COPD). Oxygen systems are set up in the home by a trained professional. If oxygen is used each caregiver must be trained to provide oxygen assistance.

> *No smoking or open flames are allowed in a home when an oxygen system is being used in the house.*

The nose piece is called a nasal cannula. It has small flexible plastic tubes that direct oxygen into the nose. It is placed in both nostrils. The tubing headband is adjusted securely around the ears. Make sure there is plenty of slack in the tubing between your person and the oxygen supply and that there are no kinks in the tubing. Monitor the oxygen therapy/system as needed throughout the day. Monitor your person's lips, skin, or fingernails looking for changes in color to blue or gray.

> *Consult your doctor, if you observe a rapid or irregular heart beat, changes in blood pressure, disorientation, drowsiness, headaches, or nausea.*

Vital Signs

Vital signs measure what is happening in a person's body. There are suggested normal values for the human body. But, each person has a baseline set of normal vital sign values unique to their body. It is important for you the caregiver to understand, measure, and record (on a routine basis) these vital signs.

> ### *Report abnormal vital signs to your doctor or home health nurse.*

Body Temperature

Body temperature is the measurement of body heat. It is normal for a person's temperature to be lower in the morning upon waking from sleep and higher in the evening after a day's activity. Some elderly loose the ability to sweat (cooling) or shiver (heating), which are the body's way of regulating temperature.

Keep a sweater or lap blanket handy to offer comfort, if your person finds the room chilly. Offer water to hydrate your person, as water helps the body regulate temperature. An elderly person's normal body temperature might be lower than 98.6 °F.

There are numerous methods to measure body temperature. Begin by purchasing and practice using a digital thermometer. This thermometer takes the temperature in a person's mouth. Your doctor might recommend a thermometer that takes the temperature in a person's ear. When you determine a normal temperature, record this information in the temperature log in the care plan notebook.

Be aware that sudden increase in body temperature indicates something is wrong. The brain can not tolerate high body temperatures. Extremely high body temperature can lead to seizures, stressing of internal organs, or even death. If you find a sudden increase, contact your doctor or home health nurse.

Respiration

Respiration is breathing and is the exchanges of oxygen and carbon dioxide used by the body. You inhale or breathe in oxygen and exhale or breathe out carbon dioxide and other gases. The typical rate is 12-20 breaths per minute. Physical activity can increase respiration, while resting can decrease it.

You can measure your person's respirations, by having them sit quietly, while watching a clock for 30 seconds and counting the number of breaths. Then, double that number to find their baseline respiration value and record it.

Sudden difficulty with breathing can panic a person. Try to calm your person down with words. Have them remain seated in their most comfortable resting position. If you know how to treat your person with inhalers for a diagnosed condition – offer the inhaler as you have been trained to do.

Observe if breathing is shallow, labored, or painful. Are their lips blue or their skin is grayish? Observe for shortness of breath or chest pains. Without leaving the person contact your doctor, home health nurse, or dial "9-1-1".

Pulse

A person's pulse is the pressure felt against the wall of the artery for each heart beat. A normal pulse is 60-80 heart beats per minute. It is important to take a person's pulse to monitor the cardiovascular system or circulation.

One method to take a person's pulse is to use the brachial artery, which is found on the inside of a person's wrist just below their thumb. Have your person rest their arm on a surface and using your index finger gently push on their wrist until you feel the pulse. You can determine the pulse rate by watching a clock for 30 seconds and counting the number of pulses; double that number to find the beats per minute.

Blood Pressure

Blood pressure is the force of the blood against the walls of the arteries. Systolic pressure is the pressure when the heart is constricting or beating. Diastolic pressure is the pressure when the heart is resting. These pressures are recorded as a fraction (systolic/diastolic), for example 120/80. Many different factors affect blood pressure. For example – age, medications, stress levels, heredity, obesity, pain levels or short term illness can alter a person's blood pressure.

Blood pressure rises and falls throughout the day. It varies depending upon whether your person has been eating, exercising, or resting. Your doctor should indicate how often and what times during the day he wants the blood pressure taken and recorded. Ask your doctor what readings he wants you to contact him immediately about.

Check with your doctor, if your person has diabetes, a shunt, poor circulation, kidney problems, a stint or pace maker, or has suffered a stroke.

You can monitor blood pressure at home using a blood pressure monitoring digital display attached to an arm or wrist cuff. If you monitor blood pressure, do not use an arm that is paralyzed, injured, swollen. Ask your doctor, nurse, or home health nurse to train you on the device you will use at home.

Take the blood pressure at the same time of day, using the same arm. Start the process by having your person sit in a comfortable position with both feet flat and the floor and arm supported on lap. Ask your person to sit still while the reading is being taken. Adjust the cuff above the elbow, with the tube (connecting to the digital display) over the center of the inside of arm. Follow instructions to inflate the cuff and obtain the reading to record. Most digital displays also indict the pulse value.

Weight

Knowing the normal weight of your person is important for many reasons. Medication doses can be based on weight. Sudden changes in weight can be a sign of an acute illness or underlying disease. Body weight depends on how active a person is. If they eat more calories than their body uses, they gain weight. If they eat too few calories, they can loose weight.

A healthy body requires a minimum amount of fat for body heat insulation, padding for the arms, legs and hips, or for stored energy for future use. But the accumulation of too much storage fat can impair movement and flexibility and increase the size of the body.

Obesity is a medical condition. Obesity is associated with many diseases, particularly heart disease, diabetes, breathing difficulties while sleeping, and osteoarthritis.

Being underweight can be the result of a mental or physical illness. Depression can account for weight loss. Look for poorly fitting dentures or sore teeth or sore gums. Being underweight is a risk factor for osteoporosis.

Regular weighing helps signal unplanned weight loss or gain. You typically measure a person's weight with a bathroom scale which reads out pounds or kilograms. 1 kilogram is approximately 2.2 pounds. Record weight and date on vital log in the care plan. Call your doctor to report unexplained weight loss.

Routine Personal Care Topics

Skin Care

Skin is the body's natural barrier. Practice routine skin assessments of your person. Check entire body for skin integrity. Look for rashes, red areas, cuts, bruises, or other injuries to the skin.

Lotion can be used to keep skin moisturized and soft. Touch can be very comforting and relaxing. Ask your person, if they would like you to provide a gentle massage of their hands, feet, arms, or legs and rub in the lotion. Gentle rubbing improved blood circulation. Always leave the skin dry.

A pressure sore is where the skin breaks down due to repetitive rubbing of a body part against another body part or bed or chair surface. Check for rashes or redness on the skin in the areas of the buttocks, back, elbows, ankles, and feet.

> ### *Notify your doctor or home health nurse immediately if you find any type of skin break down.*

If your person has a pressure sore, additional routine care to heal the sore will be needed. Ask your doctor or home health nurse to teach you the proper steps to care for the sore.

If you change a dressing on a wound, wear gloves to protect your self. Place used dressing, gloves, and other trash from the dressing change in a plastic garbage bag and dispose in the outside trash.

Infection Control

Germs – most commonly bacterial or viral – are a constant risk factor to you and your person's good health. Practicing infection control prevents germs from spreading. Read more about *Infections and Infection Control* in Chapter 1.

Wash your hands often.

Copy the next page and post near all sinks in house.

The use of additional personal protection items including using gloves, gowns, or masks help keep you the caregiver safe. Select the appropriate barrier depending upon your task. Begin by washing your hands. If barriers are needed, put them on in the following order – mask, gown, gloves. Remove them in the reverse order – gloves, gown, and mask. As you remove disposable gloves, pull them off your wrists such that they turn inside out. These items should only be used once. Discard these items in a covered trashcan that has a disposable plastic liner.

When water is not available use hand sanitizer.

Treat soiled linen or soiled clothing as infectious. Roll the soiled section to the center of the article. Keep the soiled item away from your body. Place soiled items in a separate basket, not on the floor. Wash these items separately using detergent and bleach to disinfect. Wash your hand after handling soiled items – before you handle clean items.

When you sneeze or cough, cover your mouth with the inside of you elbow. During cold and flu season, encourage everyone to cover their mouths, wash their hands, and discard any used tissue immediately.

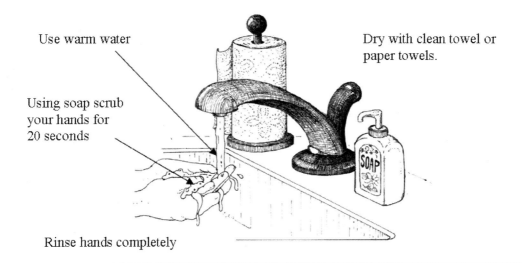

Use warm water

Dry with clean towel or paper towels.

Using soap scrub your hands for 20 seconds

Rinse hands completely

Washing hands — *Copy this page and post it near all sinks in the house.*

- Start by rinsing your hands in very warm or hot water.
- Pump 1-2 drops of liquid soap on your palms.
    - Rub your hands together to create lots and lots of soap bubbles.
    - Use each hand to completely scrub the other hand.
    - Rub all of your fingernails.
    - Scrub between your fingers
    - and on the back of your hands towards your wrists.
- The soap should be on your hands for at least 20 seconds.
- Sing the happy birthday song *twice*, as you scrub.

    - Rinse your hands by placing your wrists under the warm or hot water.
    - Scrub you hands again under the running water.
    - Let all the soap and germs rinse completely off your hands.

        - Dry your hands completely with a clean paper towel.
        - Discard this paper towel in a trash can.
        - If you choose to use cloth towels, change them frequently.

- When water is not available, use alcohol based hand sanitizers.

Non-ambulatory Personal Care

If you are caring for a person who requires you to physically help them to a standing or sitting position or a person who cannot independently move their own body, consult with your doctor, home health nurse, or physical therapist to train you in the safest methods of patient transfer. Practice these methods with the trainer. A few minutes of training and practice transfers can keep you from hurting your body or your person from falling during the transfer.

> *When a person requires complete assistance with movement from a bed, toilet, or wheelchair*
>
> *– seek help from others to help you meet caregiving needs.*

When caring for a person who is wheelchair or bed bound consider using the medical equipment available. Ask your doctor for a recommendation of what equipment might best meet your needs. There are motorized wheelchairs or scooters. Hoyer lifts mechanically lift the body from the bed to a chair or from a chair to a bed. An electric hospital-type bed can be rented or supplied by a hospice company. Adjustable bed-side tables can be rolled over the bed for eating or placed next to the bed to hold items needed by the person while they are awake. Ask for training for this equipment from the supplier while they are in your home delivering and setting it up. Keep the manuals handy for future reference.

If your bed bound person has a weak or paralyzed limb or side, consider attaching a triangle or bed-side pole. These items can be used by the strong arm to enable independence.

Be creative with bells, intercoms, or call buttons. Keep them within reach of your non-ambulatory person, so that they can easily notify you from another room or at night when they need assistance. You can find various battery operated door bells and intercoms at Radio Shack or in medical equipment catalogs.

A person who is bed bound can benefit from various pressure reducing mattresses. If s/he can not voluntarily move, follow a 2 hour body-movement rotation. Using various pillows, adjust the body in different positions to relieve pressure on the same buttocks, hips, knees, ankles, shoulders, and elbows. A lamb's wool covering might make a recliner or wheelchair softer on the body pressure points.

It is very important to keep a regular toileting schedule. Always provide immediate care for incontinence issues. Leaving the skin in a wet or soiled state places your person at increase risk of genital rashes or pressure sores.

> *Do not restrain your non-ambulatory person.*
> *Do not use bed side rails, posy belts, or a lap buddy.*
>
> *These restraints can cause injury, entrapment,*
> *or accidental death.*

If your person is not able to bear their own weight, similar benefits to exercise can be achieved with massage therapy. Gentle Swedish massage may be particularly helpful because of the long, relaxing strokes bring your person relaxation as well as promoting blood flow.

Memory Loss Care

What to look for in this section...

Memory Loss
Forms of Dementia
Progressive Stages of Alzheimer's Disease

Memory Loss and Comfort Care
General Supervision and crisis intervention
Communication and Approach

Hydration, Nutrition, Weight Monitoring

Activities of Daily Living

Safe Environments

Activities

Life Story

Behaviors
Causes behind behaviors
Managing difficult behaviors

Memory loss care is defined as comfort care.

Memory Loss

Before defining comfort care this first section discusses what is memory loss, forms of dementia and the progressive stages of Alzheimer's disease. Persons with certain types of brain tumors or a traumatic-brain-injury often experience memory loss.

A person is diagnosed with memory loss when they meet diagnostic criteria of *impaired memory, impaired thinking, judgment,* or *other mental impairment* that interferes with activities or relationships. Short term memory loss is when the person does not remember if they just ate lunch. Long term memory loss is when the person does not remember events in the past – like forgetting that their parents have died.

Persons with memory loss can become unable to:

- Make decisions about care – when to drink, eat, got to toilet
- Recognize dangerous situations – leave the stove on – forgetting they were cooking
- Ask for assistance – wonder away, become lost, and do not seek help from others
- Express their needs – used behaviors or body language rather than words
- Complete activities of daily living – such as grooming, dressing, or bathing
- Walk or communicate in anyway

Persons with memory loss need a designated person – someone who is a legal representative for living, healthcare, and financial decisions.

The *representative is responsible* for keeping the person safe, providing a safe living environment, coordinating care with others, meeting nutritional needs, providing stimulating activities and cognitive stimulation, coordinating medical care and treatments, and providing medication needs. You can be your person's caregiver and not be their representative.

Forms of Dementia

Dementia is not part of normal aging. Age-associated memory impairment is not dementia. This type of memory loss usually affects the recent memory. The person has forgetfulness, but continues to be able to use words, follow directions, reason, problem solve, and perform activities of daily living.

Dementia is multiple signs and symptoms that include the reduced ability to think, reason, and remember. Dementia is either reversible or progressive.

A person may have reversible – dementia like symptoms. There are numerous causes – depression, infection or sudden illness, stroke, nutritional deficiencies, dehydration, electrolyte imbalance, medication. The list is unending, but once the underlying cause is addressed – the person's memory improves.

There are numerous progressive dementia classifications:

- Alzheimer's Disease (AD)
- Vascular or Multi-Infarct Dementia (MID)
- AIDS
- Parkinson's Disease
- Huntington's Disease
- Multiple Sclerosis

Progressive Stages of Alzheimer's Disease

Alzheimer's disease is the most common form of dementia. Once diagnosed, a person can live 8 to 20 years or more. There is a cognitive decline over a period of years. There is a physical decline in the advanced stages.

Mild or Early Stage

- Short term memory fails - forgetfulness
- Ability to do easy and familiar tasks begin to decline
- Conversations and expressing thoughts become difficult
- Time and spatial disorientation – gets lost

Moderate or Advanced Stage

- Language skills decline
- Decrease in person's ability to make judgments – reasoning declines
- Personality changes
- Emotional outbursts
- Behaviors like agitation or wandering
- Forgets family members

Severe or Late Stage

- Becomes bed-bound
- Incontinent (bladder and bowel)
- Complete dependence
- Unresponsive to outside world

If your person is diagnosed with Alzheimer's disease – every one benefits when you connect with the Alzheimer's Association.

> *"You are not alone" – every state has a local Alzheimer's Association chapter. Find information and help at:*
>
> *www.alz.org Find us anywhere: (enter state or zip code) or call their 24/7 Helpline at 800-272-3900*

Your local chapter can offer brochures, reading lists, videos, training classes and support groups.

Memory Loss and Comfort Care

Caring for a person with Alzheimer's disease, other progressive dementia(s), age-associated dementia, or brain trauma adds an additional dimension to most topics covered in this book. If your person has memory loss – *you* -- the caregiver take on the responsibility of protecting as well as caring for your person.

Comfort care is defined as giving care with the goal of *getting the job done* while keeping your person comfortable throughout the task. Comfort care requires imaginative ways of approaching tasks. The goal is to keep your person's life as positive and fulfilling through meaningful, satisfying relationships and activities done in a nurturing and caring way.

The remainder of this section presents *adding the memory loss dimension* to caregiving. Many corresponding sections or chapters are referred to within the text of the discussion.

General Supervision and crisis intervention

General supervision of your person with memory loss goes beyond the discussion in Chapter 1. Is your person with memory loss incapable of recognizing danger, summoning assistance, expressing need or making basic care decisions? Then your person can no longer be un-supervised or left alone.

Caregivers must:

♦   Be aware of your person's location in or around the house

♦   Monitor your person's activities to ensure their health, safety, and welfare

♦   Lock-up medications and chemicals

♦   Ensure your person's medication and medical needs are met

♦   Remind your person to perform activities of daily living

♦   Remind your person of activities or appointments

Medication assistance or oversight is required as discussed in *Personal Care* and Chapter 4. It is important that you understand, monitor, and provide all medication needs of your person. Medical needs are provided according to your person's advance directives or as decided by your person's representative.

Crisis intervention can be a challenge because your person might not be able to understand or respond to verbal directions. You might have to physically direct them. If they are frightened or agitated – remain calm – using a kind voice, eye contact, and a firm grip – but get your person out of imminent danger.

> ***Do not let your person smoke – unless you are sitting with them. Keep cigarettes, lighters, and matches locked up.***

Communication and Approach

Practice the skills of good communication as discussed in Chapter 1. When communicating with your person with dementia – learn to be in their moment. Start dialog with eye contact and a smile. Say their name. Tell them your name. Use short simple sentences. Talk clear and slowly. Give them a moment to absorb what you said. Repeat the sentence. Rephrase the sentence to help them understand. Try *yes* or *no* sentences. Use nouns not pro-nouns – say *pick up the spoon* instead of *pick it up*.

When your person is speaking to you – be patient. Do not finish their sentences. Let them find their words. If they use the wrong word – do not correct them or embarrass them. Just use the correct word as you talk. For example, *I need to find the bus stop* is really *I want to sit down*. Your response – *let's find a chair so you can sit down*.

> ***Avoid correction and confrontation. Do not argue.***

Do not to argue with your person. For example, *my dad is coming today to take me home*. If you tell your person that her dad has died, that might upset her and make her sad. Instead responding – *he called you his little special girl* – will make her feel loved and happy. *Let's go look at that picture of you and your dad.*

Pay attention to clues from your person. Alzheimer's disease is a slow progressing disease – maintain communication as the disease progresses. Search for and build on your person's remaining abilities. Learn to interpret your person's behaviors. These behaviors should be viewed as attempts to communicate unmet needs. Look for basic needs -- pain, hunger, thirst, hot/cold, wet, or soiled.

Listen and teach others or visitors the best way to communicate with your person.

Realize that your person may pick-up your mood from your body language. They can sense anger, frustration, or sadness. They may feel it is their fault. Practice patience – express warmth and reassurance.

With advanced dementia your person can not tell you they are hungry, thirsty or in pain. They rely totally on you for everything. You must anticipate and respond to unspoken needs. Talk to them – while they might not respond – they might be able to understand.

Hydration, Nutrition, Weight Monitoring

Review *Supervisory Care* for hydration and nutrition and *Personal Care* for eating and monitoring weight. A confused person might forget to eat or drink – or they might be asking -- *when's lunch* -- and they ate their lunch less than 30 minutes ago. You must ensure your person eats and drinks.

Purchase a plastic pitcher with a lid that holds 2 quarts of water. Fill it every morning. If your person prefers cold water keep it in the refrigerator. Offer a drink from a glass or mug (warmed) every hour. For snacks offer other beverages. Make it a practice that your person daily drinks most of the pitcher of water. If needed limit fluids after dinner.

Watch for signs and symptoms of dehydration.

Always have your person wash their hands before eating a meal. Practice good oral hygiene to increase your person's appetite. Sit and eat with your person for meals. Watch to see if they have any trouble chewing or have mouth pain. Eating tips are discussed in *Personal Care*. Have the proper utensils, plates, and cups to encourage as much independence as possible. Give your person plenty of time to eat.

Finger foods can be used when your person does not sit still for an entire meal. Keep a plate in the refrigerator and encourage them to eat the contents between their activities. Keep snacks they like available. Provide a high protein shake once a day.

If your person eats too much – offer them low-calorie beverages or water between meals. Provide low calorie snack. Limit the sweets.

Your person's weight should be monitored every 4-5 weeks. A sudden loss of weight can signal a problem.

Activities of Daily Living

Grooming, dressing, eating, and all activities of daily living are opportunities for your person to maintain their physical, mental, communication and social skills. Help your person retain their dignity and self respect.

Guidelines:
- Respond and treat your person as an adult
- Pay attention to their needs – respond before need gets out of hand
- Maintain their privacy
- Encourage independence – expect their optimum level of functioning
- Simplify and clarify – reduce distractions – offer one item at a time
- Keep a regular routine
- Be flexible and patient

When helping your person try following these steps:

> **Break tasks into steps** that are small enough to match your person's abilities. Do they need reminding to do a task? It is time to get dressed. Do they need to have the task broken down into steps? "*Put your pants on. Do they need instructions for each task? Sit down. Put one leg in the pant. Put other leg in pant. Stand up. Pull up pants. Button the button. Zip your zipper.*"

> **Try demonstrating the step.** Go to closet – pick 2 shirts let your person choose. *Put on your shirt,* while pointing to your own shirt.

> **Help start the action.** *Button your shirt.* Start the top button for your person. Smile – put their hand on the next button.

> **Give your person time to finish the step.** If your person is able – tell them you will be back to check on them and leave the room to let them dress themselves. If they need more reminding – sit down and relax as you verbally guide their actions. If they need demonstration of each step – do not rush them. Praise each button or the final product. *Good job with that shirt!*

Using the bathroom is a private activity. When your person needs more than a reminder to use the toilet – you can back out of the room after they are on the toilet. Stay within hearing their call for help. Give them the time they need.

Bathing persons with memory loss can be a challenge. How do you get your person to not resist you? Determine their preferences. Do they like to shower or bath? Do they like hot or cooler water? You might get a spouse with memory loss to shower, by either – showering first and then telling them it is their turn *or* by joining them in the task.

Other tips to make this task more pleasant:

- Have the room warm and ready – before you get them
- Speaking in a friendly tone – *it is time to take a shower*
- Have your person soap and rinse themselves
- Use distractions – have them hold the wash rag or plastic bath toy
- Try soft music or singing as you work
- Talk to them – *doesn't this warm water feel nice?*
- If you help – begin with the back, arms, and legs – moving to the front or Perineal-area last.
- Wash their hair last.
- Don't let them get cold – have a big fluffy towel ready.

A word about mirrors in bathrooms – *occasionally* – persons with dementia look into the mirror and think there is another person (who they do not know) is in the bathroom with them. If this bothers your person – cover the mirrors so they can not see their reflections. On the other hand – if they enjoy talking to the person in the mirror – what harm does that cause?

Safe Environments

Using directional signs might prove useful if your person is confused. Use a large card and a black marker to make labels for ***bedroom – bathroom – kitchen***. Smaller signs can be taped on drawers or cabinets for – ***socks – clean towels –plates/cups/silverware***.

Safety proofing the house and outdoors means storing or removing items that might harm your person. Review Chapter 2 to get general ideas for making the house safe. Read all labels of products found in the home and act accordingly for those with the warning about **"KEEP OUT OF REACH OF CHILDREN"**. Consider using baby locks on laundry room and garage or storage cabinets.

As general supervision – you must now monitor your person when they cook, smoke, use the bathroom, or spend time outdoors. Monitoring does not mean you have to shadow or be with your person, you just have to be aware of what they are doing and ensure their activity brings benefit – not harm.

If your person begins to wander – this is when your person gets up and walks around with a purpose. This purpose may not be stated or reasonable to you – *I'm off to pick up the children from school* – when the children are actually grown and living in a different state. Get an identification bracelet or necklace made with your person's name, your phone number, and a simple description like – *I have memory loss*. This identification lets others become involved more quickly and can bring your person safely home.

Chapter 2 discusses using locks on doors. You need to balance the safety of your person. Does placing a lock on the exit door to keep you person from leaving the house alone – also keep your person from leaving the house when there is a fire? Consider solutions that work for both daily and emergency situations – such as putting alarms on doors and windows.

Activities

Your person may have lost the ability to spontaneously plan what household chores, exercise, recreational or social activities they enjoy. But once set to task – they are ready and able to succeed. Comfort care includes making your person productive and keeping them physically, mentally and creatively active.

> *Activities enhance your person's self esteem – offering independence, joy and purpose.*

Review *Supervisory Care* – create an *Activity List* – list everything your person is capable of doing and enjoys doing. Add activities that include family and friends. The *Palliative Care* section *Meaningful Activities* presents ideas for hobbies and collections, reminiscing, picture albums, and getting out of the house.

Buy books with specific activities for persons with Alzheimer's disease. Add new activities to the list – as you discover them. Keep this activity list and include these activities when you update the monthly event or activity calendar.

> *Post this month's Event Calendar and Activity List on the refrigerator or bulletin board.*
>
> *File past calendars with the care plan.*

Productivity

What did your person do? A banker or accountant – can they still balance their checkbook? Find games that use numbers like UNO or Yahtzee. A pharmacist – do they enjoy looking at the drug ads in magazines? A homemaker – can they still vacuum the carpets, dust the furniture, or fold the laundry?

As part of the daily routine – have your person set the table before meals, help with dishes after the meal, feed the dog or check for the mail. Praise and thank them for their help.

Exercise

Some amount of exercise each day is good. Is there an exercise tape/DVD you and your person can follow along with? Check out your local bookstore for types of exercise that fit your person's needs – like exercises done from a chair. What about dancing? Find music that encourages your person to move to the beat. Skip exercise on days with doctor appointments, outings, or visitors coming to the house.

Does your person enjoy walking – walk around the block together. For variety – take your person to the local park. Take your person to watch local elementary school football or soccer games. Go to the zoo each fall. Trips to the mall or grocery store combine walking and purpose.

Invest in Wii Sports- Baseball, Golf, or Bowling

Play this TV game standing or sitting. Challenge the grandkids for family fun.

Recreational

Daily recreational activities keep routine and fun in your person's life. Recreation encourages socialization. Do activities in a comfortable and adult setting. Play in a room without other distractions.

Choose activities based on your person's past and present interests, abilities and functional levels, and time of day. Obtain picture books, magazines, or activity books available for use. Encourage your person to share their thoughts as you read the text or look at the pictures. Puzzles (with larger pieces) can be purchased with pictures of past-times, animals, or objects. Find a puzzle of the United States (one piece per state) and discuss facts about states. Reminisce about past family vacations.

Games can provide quiet activity. Determine which games your person enjoys – bingo, dominos, Kings in the Corners. Change the rules to fit your person's mental abilities. Do not keep score. Enjoy their enjoyment.

Social

Many of the above activities are social – your person is interacting with you. If you are the primary caregiver for your person – consider enlisting others in providing a *social break* for your person. This break can be a visit in your home. You the caregiver leave the house or do something for yourself – like talking on the phone with a friend or reading a book or the newspaper.

> *Consider enrolling your person at an Adult Day Health Care Center (see Supervisory Care) 2-3 mornings a week.*

Life Story

A life story is a tool to help when your person has dementia, Alzheimer's disease, or age-associated memory loss. The information is used by caregivers or volunteers caring for your person. It helps those who do not know your person. A life story is usually one page in length and kept handy by the bed or in the care plan. It gives the caregivers insight to your person. It brings your person respect and dignity.

You write your person's life story to give clues used to communicate, plan activities, and distractions to use while giving providing routine care.

A life story can include:

- List some of your person's favorite things to talk about
- Your person's favorite music or radio station
- Other things a caregiver needs to know…

> *Review the Activity List with new caregivers or visiting friends and family.*

My name is…	I like to be called…	age …	birthday…
Val Jerome H.	Jerry	82	September 17th

My wife's name is…	Children… Suzanne, Elizabeth (lives close),
Barbara	Patrick, and Betsy

Grand Children…

Benjamin (navy) and sister Alicia (teacher)

Corina (visits often – HS junior volleyball, cross country)

Jesse (trade school) and brother Joshua (loves dogs)

Nina (youngest – seven – loves school)

Pictures by bed…

Barbara on porch chair	4 adult children
Betsy's glamour-shot	Nina with Daisy (dog)
Benjamin (uniform)	Jerry sitting beside model train

Birth place…	Parents…	Living siblings…
Eastland, Texas	Celia and Chester	sisters: Joyce and Judy

My interests…

I enjoy model trains – one is set-up in garage

I enjoy gardening, sitting in chair on patio watching birds and squirrels

I enjoy watching base-ball on the TV. I am a Diamondback fan

I love talking about and visiting with my grandchildren

My special care needs…

I use hearing aids – look at me when you speak

I need to eat puréed foods and use a straw to drink liquids

I need to be reminded to use the bathroom every 2 hours.

I am able to use the bathroom – unaided.

I enjoy playing "Kings in the Corners" in the afternoon for 30 minutes

Favorite foods, beverages, snacks …

ice-water, chocolate or vanilla ice cream, coffee with breakfast

My name is…	I like to be called…	age …	birthday…

My wife's name is…	Children…

Grand Children…

Pictures by bed…

Birth place…	Parents…	Living siblings…

My interests…

My special care needs…

Favorite foods, beverages, snacks …

Family Pictures

Like the life story, placing or hanging familiar family pictures where your person can see them -- gives you or other caregivers topics to talk about.

Ideas for pictures are:

- Current pictures of family and friends - especially those who can not be with your person on a regular basis (live out of state)
- Pictures of your person as a child
- Pictures from your person's past, like their parents, children, neighbors, friends
- Events - weddings, anniversaries, birthdays
- Vacation pictures with them or family members in the picture
- Past pets or pets that were given away

Many people with memory loss keep their long term memories for a longer time. The may have forgotten that their mother died, but they can remember that she made the best blueberry cobblers.

Family pictures are also very useful when the far away person calls on the phone. It is helpful to have their pictures in front of your person while they talk.

To help unfamiliar caregivers label the pictures with names, dates, relationships, or places (sister, Marie who lives in Manitou Springs, Colorado).

Behaviors

Every person is unique. The same can be stated for your person's journey deeper into dementia. At various times your person may experience any or several of the following challenging behaviors.

Aggression	Hiding / Hoarding	Resistive
Agitation	Insulting	Rummaging
Combative	Jealousy	Screaming / yelling
Delusions	Paranoia	Shadowing / following
Demanding	Pacing	Sun-downing
Depression	Repetitive actions	Wandering
Hallucinations	Repetitive questions	Withdrawal

> ***Your person can not control their behaviors.***
> ***Your person's disease or injury causes brain damage that impairs their thinking, judgment, memory or functioning.***

Causes behind behaviors

If you understand what causes these behaviors, you can better understand that your person is not behaving this way on purpose. Look for the meaning and purpose behind the behaviors.

Possible causes of behaviors:

<u>Physical discomfort</u>

- ♦ Needs to use bathroom, hunger, thirst, uncomfortable clothing
- ♦ Impaired vision or hearing – causing misunderstandings
- ♦ Has pain, illness, tired
- ♦ Needs to move or exercise

*Consult with a doctor, if you think your person is in pain,
sick, or has an urine infection.*

Physical environment

 ♦ Room is cluttered, confusing, unfamiliar

 ♦ Room is noisy, too hot or cold, too light or dark

 ♦ Confining or large open room

 ♦ Changes in routine

Other people

 ♦ Being in a crowded room, to much happening around them

 ♦ Does not know person talking to them

 ♦ Does not understand the person talking to them

 ♦ Caregiver's body language is negative, sad, or threatening

 ♦ Caregiver's behavior – anger, scolding, invading person's privacy

Emotional

 ♦ Feels lost, threatened, insecure

 ♦ Emotional reactions to any of the above causes

 ♦ Feels trapped or confined

 ♦ Stressed for any reason

 ♦ Feels useless, bored, sad, scared, angry

 ♦ Desires touch, comfort, reassurance

Prevent the behavior by anticipating and meeting comfort needs of your person. Create a calming and familiar environment in the house. Keep the temperature comfortable for your person. Follow a daily routine that blends needed tasks (like grooming, eating, and bathroom) with stimulating and meaningful activities that help your person feel useful (see *Activity* section). Balance quiet or sitting activities, exercise, and rest periods – being aware of your person's responses.

Approach your person with a gentle approach, smile, go slow, talk in simple sentences, and show warm, compassionate body language.

Managing difficult behaviors

The goal when interacting with your person and any difficult behavior is to address their safety, comfort, and respond to them as an individual. When addressing the difficult behavior keep your approach gentle and keep your emotions calm.

Try managing behaviors with distractions. Offer your person something to eat or drink. Offer them something to hold – a stuffed animal, a pillow, or your hand. Offer them something to look at – a card, a picture book, or a family picture album. Talk about topics your person likes to hear about.

If your person is agitated, yelling, hitting, or resisting...

1. Remove your person from the stressful situation.
2. Do not let them hurt you – back away
3. Give them a hug – compliment them
4. Have them sit in a comfortable chair in a quiet room.
5. Try using rocking, holding hands, or playing soothing music.
6. Then introduce a distraction to refocus your person.

Talk with your person's doctor if behaviors of depression, delusion, or hallucinations begin occurring – or if you suspect pain may be causing a behavior.

Palliative Care

What to look for in this section...

Palliative Care Goals

Physical Comfort

Pain Management

Breathing Problems

Digestive Problems

Skin Irritation

Meaningful Activities

Hobbies / Reminiscing / Picture Therapy / Food

Getting out of the house

Looking ahead and life-time dreams

Meaningful activities for Advanced Dementia

Life Story

Emotional and Spiritual Needs

Surroundings / Pets / Emotional Responses

Communicating / Health Updates

Spiritual

Hospital Stays

Hospice

Palliative care is defined as care provided to persons with either a serious or terminal illness of any kind.

Palliative care maximizes quality of life, identifies and treats physical or emotional pain and other forms of discomfort, and is sensitive to your person's social and emotional well-being.

It can be end of life care. When you visit friends or family in Hospice you witness palliative care.

Throughout this book dignity – self-determination – privacy – choice are stressed in every step of caregiving. When you provide palliative care – you must find ways to meet the *spoken or un-spoken* needs of your person.

Palliative care topics can be applied to any level of caregiving – your person can benefit – making their world a more comfortable place. Take an idea and bend it to apply to your person's specific situation.

Palliative Care Goals

Your person's unique diagnosis and health care directives determine the goals of palliative care. The care requires an awareness and respect of your person. The goal is to enhance your person's quality of life while providing basic care such as feeding, bathroom or incontinent care, and mobility assistance.

When your person is able to communicate, discuss with your person their wishes and expectations of their remaining days. Involve others – *palliative care is a group effort*. Seek outside help – begin with family and friends, consider hiring another caregiver, bring in a church member or trained counselor to help with loss and grief, speak with your doctor about pain management in the home setting.

Advance dementia – advanced brain tumors – traumatic-brain-injury Is your person severely confused and perhaps bed-bound? They may not make demands or voice complaints – but do you provide them with quality recreational and social interactions?

End-stage of terminal illness   Is your person in the end-stage of cancer, emphysema, kidney failure, Parkinson's or any of many other illnesses or diseases? This stage may rob them of physical strength or body movement – or bring them nausea, loss of appetite, breathlessness, or fatigue. Your person may need emotional or spiritual healing to help them deal with their death.

Stroke   Has your person had a stroke?   A stroke can leave your person mentally alert with loss of speech and other bodily functions, as well as varying degrees of paralysis of different parts of their body. This sudden physical change can bring agitation, anger, or sadness – which need compassionate responses.

Coma   Is your person in a coma? A person in a coma is unable to move and does not respond to their environment. Actions and words used when caring for your person in a coma – should be the same as if they could hear you and respond to your touch.

Physical Comfort

Your person can be physically uncomfortable for many reasons. Now is the time to ensure your person is as free of pain and other symptoms as possible.

Pain Management

Serious pain is common in most terminally ill people. If your person says they are in pain or they indicate they are in pain, they have the right to receive effective pain management. Struggling with pain can be draining for both your person and yourself.

Watch for these symptoms:

♦ <u>Facial expressions</u> – grimacing, frownin9g, frightened, tears in eyes

♦ <u>Mood</u> – irritability, confusion, withdrawal, agitation, aggressiveness

♦ <u>Body language</u> – clenched fists, restlessness, rubbing, holding, or guarding body part, rocking, physically abusive, resists care, noisy breathing

♦ <u>Vocal</u> – asks for help, moaning, grunting, whining, calling out, screaming, crying, verbally abusive

♦ <u>Behaviors</u> – appetite change, refuses food, sleep patterns change, sudden stop in common routines

Good pain management improves quality of life. Talk with your person's doctor about their pain. Give the medication as prescribed. Pain is easier to prevent than to relieve – overwhelming pain is hard to manage. Try to make sure that the level of pain does not *get ahead* of the pain relieving medicines. If the pain is not controlled – ask your doctor for a consultation with a pain management specialist. Hospice agencies provide medication for pain management.

Try these other methods to help reduce pain:

♦ Heat relaxes muscles – use warm showers, baths, warm wash cloths, occasional heated therapy wrap

♦ Gently massage sore spots, transcutaneous electrical nerve stimulation (TENS)

♦ Gentle movements, stretches, exercise, aquatics

♦ Cooling the skin and muscles – cool wash cloth, occasional ice pack or chilled therapy wrap

♦ Use extra pillows, soft seat cushions, foot rests

♦ Imagery, breathing and body relaxation techniques, biofeedback

♦ Compassionate responses, soft caresses, holding your person, quiet surroundings, very soft music

♦ Enjoyable activities – distractions can take your person's mind off the pain

Breathing Problems

Your person might experience shortness of breath or the feeling that breathing is difficult. Worrying about their next breath can make it hard for them to have conversations or meaningful visits. Try rising the head of the bed by putting long cut boards or stable cider-blocks under the top bed posts or bed frame. Using a room vaporizer can help. Their doctor may suggest starting your person on oxygen therapy to help this discomfort.

Digestive Problems

Radiation treatment and various medication therapies can result in the lack of saliva. A dry mouth and throat can lead to chewing, swallowing, or speaking difficulties for your person. Ice chips can make your person more comfortable or using a flexible straw with beverages. Thickening products for liquids are available to make swallowing easier. Seek help from your doctor or a Registered Dietitian about a special diet of soft or pureed food can address the chewing or swallowing issues.

Some pain medication can cause loss of appetite, nausea, vomiting, or constipation. For loss of appetite, try offering favorite foods in small amounts. Offer nutritional supplement shakes. Do not force your person to eat. Inform your person's doctor about these symptoms as there are medications that help control nausea or vomiting or constipation.

If your person is very near death, losing their appetite is a common and normal part of dying. A conscious decision to give up food can be part of your person's acceptance that death is near. Going without food and/or water is generally not painful to a dying person. Feeding tubes and IV fluid hydration may be specifically addressed in your person's advanced directives.

Skin Irritation

Skin problems can be very uncomfortable. Read *Personal Care* to review routine *Skin Care* and a discussion about pressure sores. Keeping the skin clean and moisturized is important. Keep bottles of alcohol-free lotion beside the bed and in daytime rooms. Apply lip balm to dry lips. Place a warm wash cloth over closed eyes or use wetting eye drops to relieve dry eyes.

Sitting or lying in one position puts constant pressure on sensitive skin. Turning your person from side to back and to their other side can help prevent skin breakdown or pressure sores. Use foam pads or pillows to adjust the body and protect heels, hips, or elbows. A special *air-pressure-motion* (medical) mattress, egg-crate foam, a wool-lamb skin or chair cushion can help relieve pressure.

Follow these guidelines when giving your person a bath in the bed.

Bed Bathing Guidelines

A towel bath is used when your person refuses to shower or bath – or is non-ambulatory.

1. Place a large beach towel (fan folder) and 4 washcloths in a large garbage bag.

2. Dilute 1-2 oz of no-rinse soap in 2 quarts warm (110°F) water.

3. Warm a second beach towel in microwave for drying. Roll warmed beach towel in another towel.

4. Place these items near bed.

5. Undress your person in the bed, but keep them covered with a top blanket.

6. Pour soapy water into bag, massage water into towels. Towels/clothes should be wet - not saturated.

7. Take the fan folded beach towel begin at the feet,   unfolding up their body – moving the top blanket off – keeping your person covered at all times.

8. Begin washing the body by massaging the towel. Use washcloths to wash

    (1) underarms, under breasts,
    (2) perineal area, and
    (3) face.
    (4) Roll your person on their sides to wash - back and buttocks.

9. Begin at the feet with the dry warm beach towel, unfolding up their body – removing wet towel.

10. Give a light massage with lotion – let your person enjoy a nap before re-dressing them.

Meaningful Activities

Meaningful activities distract your person from their medical situations. Activity can improve self-esteem, bring happiness, reduce stress, and enrich relationships. Many of these suggested activities also help your person through a *life review* – helping them realize their life has made an impact on their loved ones and society.

Hobbies and Collections

Does your person have a hobby or a collection? Seek ways to do the hobby in a meaningful way. Spend time looking at and talking about their baseball card or coin collections. Start a new collection – buy a coin book and fill in the state commemorative quarters (1999-2008). Discuss interesting state information.

Reminiscing

Find *coffee table* (large picture books) about subjects that interest your person – like gardening, horses, trains, etc. Find travel books about states or countries you person has lived in or visited. Join your local library or check out used book stores. As you look at these books together – encourage your person to tell you stories.

Creating a *Life Story book – Memories from the Past...* can be a meaningful activity for a dying person to tell and give to their grandchildren or nieces and nephews. It can include stories that even you the caregiver might not have heard before. Ask your person open ended questions like - tell me about your time in the military. As they tell their story encourage them to tell more details. Let them talk about their childhood, occupations, family life, or travels. Use a tape recorder and later type out the stories.

Picture Therapy

A picture is worth a thousand words. Dig in the closet for those dusty boxes or pull the picture albums off the shelf. Spend time looking at pictures. Let your person reminisce about their lives when the pictures were taken. Write the names of the people and date taken – on the back of the picture.

Create a special bedside photo album of your person's favorite pictures. Add captions with explanations of people, places, and dates of photos. Let your person share these album and stories with other visitors.

Get out the camera and snap pictures of your person with visitors. Ask others to take pictures of you and your person – especially at family gatherings or special outings. Keep these in frames for daily viewing.

Food

Did your person enjoy cooking? Look for the box or drawer of their favorite recipes. Locate their favorite cook books from the shelf. Does your person enjoy eating? Let your person suggest recipes they would like you to make. If you are not a cook – call in other family or friends to copy the recipe and prepare special meals. Create a *Grandma's Favorite Recipes* book for grandchildren.

Add your person's favorite foods to the menu. Meals need to be smaller and snacks offer often. Offer soft and sweet snacks like pudding, ice cream, cut fruit, sweetened yogurt, and peanut butter sandwiches.

The smell of baking cookies can stimulate the appetite and be a fun afternoon activity. If possible, have your person sitting at the dining table. They can help measure, mix, and put cookies on the baking sheet. Offer these treats to visitors – allowing your person the pleasure of giving instead of receiving.

Getting out of the house

Break the daily routine. When your person is able – getting out of the house can lift everyone's spirits. Involve others in the outing if you are not comfortable going alone.

> **Get a handicap placard for the car – many parking lots have close-up reserved handicap parking spaces.**

Places to go:

- A walk around the block or push your person's wheelchair as you walk
- A trip to the grocery store or pharmacy
- Lunch or dinner at the local diner
- An afternoon movie
- Local family visits, dinners, or gatherings
- Favorite parks, lakes, or even the front or back porch

> **Consider having your person spend a few days with family or friends – at their homes.**

Looking ahead and life-time dreams

Celebrate future events – for example, if your person's 50th wedding anniversary is approaching, have the celebration sooner. This allows your person to share the event – seeing old friends, eating the cake, and taking that special picture. The same goes for an early Easter Sunday or Christmas holiday festivities.

Often life has gotten in the way of fulfilling that life-time dream of traveling to Hawaii, cruising to Alaska or the Caribbean, staying at a beach-front hotel, or attending a game at the stadium of a favorite team. If your person expresses a desire to go on a final trip – make it happen. Take pictures to bring home.

Meaningful Activities for Advanced Dementia

When your person has advanced dementia make all activities – even dressing, bathing, grooming – a safe, comfortable, and positive experience. Connect with them in a meaningful way.

Somehow stimulate their senses so that they show signs of awareness, appreciation, and enjoyment. They may make brief eye contact, express a subtle smile, or relax. Find that unique connecting point that makes your person feel both stimulated and soothed.

Effective actions:

- talk to them with a soothing pleasant voice
- looking them in the eye and smiling
- use touch frequently (unless they do not like touch)
- brief massages – especially to the hands and feet with lotion
- humming or singing a song – saying a familiar prayer
- offer them a favorite food
- giving them a stuffed bear or baby doll to cuddle
- taking them outside – or seating them near a window to look outside
- balance stimulating and calming activities

Life Story

The life story is introduced in *Memory Loss*. In palliative care it can be used when your person is unable to communicate due to stroke or disease as well as when your person has advanced dementia or age-associated memory loss.

You write your person's life story to give clues used to communicate, plan palliative activities, and distractions to use while giving providing routine care. Have caregivers or volunteers who do not know your person – review the life story of your person with you.

Emotional and Spiritual Needs

This section presents the concept of *creature comforts*. Where your person spends their waking hours during the day – what words are spoken – what thoughts are thought – sharing with others. These are the emotional and spiritual needs.

Surroundings

Comfort care uses surroundings instead of environment – a comfortable and comforting place. Things your person sees and touches need to be soft, warm, safe, and familiar.

The bed needs a good mattresses, soft mattress pad, sheets, and pillows. Use comforters/afghans that are familiar or special to your person. Have a recliner or comfortable chair in the bedroom. Have a guest chair by the bed for visitors. Place a nightstand or hospital table close to the bed – keeping frequently used items like Kleenex, lip balm, reading glasses, and water glass handy.

Windows need draperies/blinds that can be opened to allow your person to see the yard and blue sky outside. Be able to darken the room during the day when your person is resting. If your person reads in that room – put a reading light by the bed or chair.

Decorate the walls with favorite or recent pictures. Put a *close line* of cards and hand-drawn pictures from the grand children on a wall. Keep books or a photo album on the dresser. Flowers (silk or real) often bring a smile. Have a *boom-box* to play CDs or tapes of relaxing music.

If your person is ambulatory – bring this comforting pattern to the room where they spend their time during the day. Have a TV available. Place a recliner or comfortable chair in the room. Place an end-table near the chair for more Kleenex, lip balm, hand lotion, and water glass. Keep a basket of recent cards from well-wishers. Order their favorite magazines. Keep a spare lap blanket nearby.

Create a place on a sheltered (outside) porch or near a low inside window that allows your person to enjoy the blue sky – be warmed by the sunshine – listen to the birds or watch squirrels or garden area.

Pets

A pet can bring therapeutic benefit to your person. A pet can be a dog, a cat, parakeet, or gold fish. You know this if there has been a pet living in the house while you have been caregiving.

Benefits of a Pet:

- A pet gives your person a reason to get out of bed each day.
- A pet can decrease the chance of depression and increase socialization.
- A pet can prevent loneliness.
- A pet provides unconditional, nonjudgmental love and affection.
- Pets are good listeners – often offering the benefit of a purr or a lick on the hand.
- Cats and fish are interesting to watch.
- Pets live in the moment.

When a pet does not live in the house, find people who will bring *appropriate* pets for frequent visits.

Emotional

Tell your person that you love them. Reinforce your feelings of care and concern – often. Touch your person – hold hands, caress their arm, kiss and hug them. Laugh about things. Do not be afraid to play (between caregiving).

Your person may need to find peace by resolving unsettled issues with friends or family. This may lead to taking care of unfinished business, putting affairs in order, and deepening existing relationships. They may wish to spend more time with friends or family. Depending upon your person's wishes – do not limit visits.

Visits are a two way street – they allow others to spend time with your person and your person gets to hear different news or an interesting story. Visitors can share their feelings for your person. They can tell your person how special they are and reminisce past times together.

> *Visitors can be welcome breaks for you to spend time away from your person.*

When you do leave the house – tell your person where you are going and when you will return.

Communicating Health Updates

Keeping in touch with a number of concerned and caring friends or a large family can be stressful for a primary caregiver. Repeating the same details to each caller can be time consuming. Set up an e-mail account as a non-disruptive way to communicate. You can respond at convenient times. You can send one message to a list of friends and family. Have a family member set up a website where friends and family can share news, pictures, thoughts, and wishes.

Another easy way to communicate regular or daily news about your person's condition or hospital stay is by leaving a current message on your voice mail greeting. For example – *you have reached Mary's home phone. Today is Tuesday. Walter is still in ICU – but he is breathing much better since the antibiotics beginning to help his pneumonia.*

Spiritual

Addressing spiritual concerns at the end of life can be as vital as pain relief or comfort care for your person. Spirituality can help them find meaning to their suffering. Spirituality can find hope in the mist of despair. Let your person talk about topics that are important to them. If they want to talk about dying – sit down and listen to their thoughts.

Questions of the dying:

- Why did this happen to me?...What will happen to me when my life ends?

- Why would God allow me to suffer like this?...

- Will I be remembered? Will I be missed?

Does your person miss going to church? At their request, you can arrange for visitors from their church or for communion to be brought to the house after Sunday services. Many religions televise their services on Sunday morning. Some churches record their services on tapes to be listened to at home or publish the text of the Sunday sermon on their web page.

Read scripture verses or share prayers together. Have a friend visit to sing hymns and pray with your person. Play instrumental church hymns while you relax. There are local radio stations that broadcast bible programs and religious music.

Hospital Stays

Your person might experience an acute illness (like pneumonia), fall, or other disease related medical emergency or surgery that requires a hospital stay. This event can result in the need for temporary or permanent long-term nursing care. If your person wants to come home *and* you and the family are able to provide palliative care – there are *Home and Community Based Services* that can provide additional help (for payment) and can train you the primary caregiver the new needed healthcare delivery skills. If your person is unable to independently move their bodies review *Non-ambulatory Personal Care.*

Ask your hospital discharge planner to give you information about:

- Home health aide and home health nursing agencies

- Physical, occupational , and speech therapy (home-based) services

- Medical equipment supply agencies... Hospice agencies

When you – the caregiver – are placed in the position of providing palliative care to your person – you need assistance with this 24/7 care demand. You also need assistance in coping with your stress and maintaining your own health.

Hospice

Hospice care is compassionate care provided to persons facing a terminal illness or injury. The underlying goal of hospice is to allow your person to die with palliative care and without pain. Treatments and medications are for palliative care – not a medical cure. Speak with your doctor if you have questions about hospice.

Hospice care can be provided in a home setting. Hospice in-patient facilities are also available, if your person needs around the clock care. These facilities can also provide respite to families who need a short-term break from caregiving. The cost of hospice care is usually covered by Medicare, Medicaid, and most medical insurances.

A doctor oversees the hospice team. An initial exam and assessment is done. A nurse visits the home, as needed and makes arraignments for the medications and medical equipment (such as an electric hospital bed). A caregiver can be scheduled a few hours each week, as needed to provide personal care services. A social worker can be assigned to address legal, financial, and emotional issues. If requested, a chaplain can address spiritual concerns.

The hospice team deals with your person and the entire family's needs. The hospice agency can also provide bereavement or grief counselors to assist the caregiver and family after the death with one-on-one counseling or support groups, if desired.

Fundamentals of Caregiving
This part of the book applies to all levels of care.

Caregiving Basics

> This chapter introduces several basic caregiver tools that are necessary for all levels of caregiving. Communication, infection and infection control, food prep and storage are used on a daily basis. General supervision covers the broader topics of over seeing medication and medical needs, crisis intervention, and reporting abusive situations. Caregiving requires an awareness of stress, grief or loss, and depression.

Communication

Communication is a process of sharing information. Methods of communication can include observation or watching, effective listening, a verbal conversation, or a non-verbal action like a smile, a frown, or a caring touch. Messages sent or received are influenced by the way the message is expressed.

> *Awareness of your person's values or background and showing respect to your person improves communication.*

When using verbal communication, be sure you have the attention of your person. Good eye contact helps communication. Speak in a clear, lower tone, slow voice. Use words that your person understands. Tone, inflection, and loudness can change the meaning of your message. Restate your sentence using different words if you think your directions are not understood.

When you are encouraging a two-way conversation, use open ended sentences that require more than a simple yes or no answer. For example – *"tell me how you are feeling today."* Give your person time to think and respond. Be quiet. Be an effective listener. Let your person speak. Show interest in their reply. Repeat what you heard or continue the conversation from the response you hear. Find topics to discuss that interest your person.

When you need specific information, use clarifying questions or statements. Ask short, direct yes or no questions. Restate their response in clear and simple words. Ask the question with different words if you get a vague or unclear response.

Non-verbal communication can happen with or without verbal communication. Examples of non-verbal communication are facial expression, eye contact, body position, or touching the person. A smile or a hug shows warmth, comfort or reassurance. Sitting down with a person indicates your willingness to share. Folding your arms, pointing your finger, shaking your head no, might indicate you are not happy with the person. Do not read, look away, or turn your back when speaking or listening to your person. Give them your full attention.

Using touch during communication can strengthen interactions. Touch should be spontaneous. Touch can establish your presence and reassurance or interest. Touch can also indicate your availability to your confused person or person with hearing loss or loss of sight. Do not sneak-up on your person, use your voice first and then continue with a gentle initial touch.

General Supervision

General supervision is a key element of caregiving. As a caregiver, you have a responsibility to be aware of what is happening – on a continual or regular basis. General supervision of the person and their living environment ensures that the needs of the person are met at all times. It is also your responsibility to act and communicate with the appropriate people when the need is beyond your abilities.

General supervision can be as simple as monitoring your person's home environment, nutritional or social needs, frequent communication with your person when he or she lives alone, or being available for occasional transportation needs. General supervision also includes meeting medication and medical needs, providing crisis intervention during an emergency, accident, incident, illness, or significant change, and finally being proactive if you suspect abuse, neglect, or exploitation.

Medication and Medical Needs

Frequent discussions about medical conditions, concerns or needs, and actual medication being taken by your person are required. These discussions offer helpful, if not life-saving assistance to your person. Medical concerns or condition might require a visit to the doctor. A medical need, like purchase of a cane or a walker can be obtained by a caregiver. Medication errors can be avoided with a careful review of current medications taken.

If your person is independent and requires no assistance, there still needs to be open communication. This person knows what medications they take, what medical conditions they have and are capable of handling their own needs. Encourage your person to tell you when a new condition occurs or a new medication is started.

Providing medication assistance to a person taking medication might include:

♦ Obtaining medication from pharmacy or drug store

♦ Storing medication

♦ Reading the medication label

♦ Setting up the medication organizer

♦ Reminding the person that it is time to take a medication

♦ Opening the medication container

♦ Pouring or placing the specified dosage into a container or into the resident's hand

♦ Creating or completing the medication log sheet

Providing assistance for medical conditions, needs, or concerns depends upon the specific situation. You might be able to be trained to provide the assistance, such as take the blood pressure of the person. Driving the person to the doctor's office or coordinating professional services of a nurse or physical therapist visiting the home are also examples of providing assistance for a medical condition or need.

Medication administration means the application of medication to its ultimate destination on the body of the person. Medication administration might include:

♦ Placing a pill in the person's mouth

♦ Injecting insulin into your person's leg or body

♦ Placing a suppository into their rectum

Medical care at home is usually given by trained professionals such as nurses, physical therapists, or hospice staff.

Medication Services **(Chapter 1)** *expands on medication lingo and providing assistance with medications.*

Crisis intervention

Crisis intervention is when you determine conditions of **imminent danger** to life, health or safety of your person or caregiver.

Examples of imminent danger include:

♦ an emergency, such as a fire in the home or a possible stroke

♦ an accident, such as a fall or a deep cut from a sharp object

♦ an incident, such as reporting your person with memory loss missing from the home

♦ an illness, such as a high body temperature and severe vomiting

♦ a significant change, such as sudden confusion from a adverse medication reaction

♦ finding your person in an abusive or neglected situation

Review (Chapter 3) When there is an Emergency for more ideas.

Depending upon the crisis – your job is to provide an **immediate response** of help to your person to prevent imminent harm or to stabilize or resolve a physical health or psychosocial health issue of your person.

Remain calm.

Get help.

Get your person to a safe place.

Abuse, Neglect, or Exploitation

Older persons who are unable to care for themselves may be in danger of abuse, neglect, or financial exploitation. Because of physical or mental impairment, these vulnerable adults are unable to protect themselves. Elder domestic violence victims often do not talk about or admit to abuse, neglect, or financial exploitation from family members.

*As a relative, friend, or caregiver –
there are things you can do to stop elder abuse:*

- Learn to spot the signs of elder abuse.

- Educate yourself and others on how to prevent it.

- Recognize the problem by reporting it.

Definitions

Abuse is:

- intentional infliction of physical harm

- injury caused by negligent acts or omissions

- unreasonable confinement

- sexual abuse or sexual assault

- emotional abuse

Emotional abuse is repeatedly:

- ridiculing or demeaning a vulnerable adult

- making derogatory remarks to a vulnerable adult

- verbally harassing a vulnerable adult

- threatening to inflict physical or emotional harm on a vulnerable adult

Neglect is a pattern of conduct without a person's informed consent resulting in deprivation of:

♦ food or water

♦ medication or medical services

♦ shelter with adequate cooling or heating

♦ services necessary to maintain minimum physical or mental health

Exploitation is the illegal or improper use of an incapacitated or vulnerable adult or his resources for another's profit or advantage.

Prevention

In order to prevent elder abuse or neglect, we first have to look at the profile of the typical abusers. Most often, they are caregivers in some capacity, usually a family member. Perhaps the family member *inherited* the task of caregiving and is ill prepared or trained to provide caregiving. If the caregiver is elderly themselves, they physically cannot provide the care that is needed for ailing spouses or parents. Elders living alone may *unintentionally* cause self-neglect due to numerous reasons.

> *Whatever the reason—elder abuse, neglect, or exploitation cannot and should not be ignored.*

Be alert to the signs of neglect. Be observant of nutrition, hydration, food in the house, appearance of the person, cleanliness and up-keep of the home, and temperature of the home. Review medications and ask the caregiver and the person receiving care questions about their daily life.

Listen to what is being said. Do you hear any emotional abuse? Look for any physical signs of abuse, such as bruises, sores, or broken bones. Speak with the elder without the caregiver present. Does the elder show signs of fear or distrust of the caregiver? Do not rely on a caregiver known or suspected to have alcohol or substance abuse issues.

Families can be very secretive about their finances. The illegal use of a person's Social Security check, savings, or credit cards is exploitation or financial abuse. Fraud schemes, scams, and con games often target the elderly. Observation and good communication are keys to avoid financial loss.

Advanced planning through the use of health care, mental health, or financial powers of attorney (POA) and advance directives are presented in Chapter 6. If the person living alone is a vulnerable or incapacitated adult without legal advanced planning documents, it may become necessary for the county court-system to appoint a suitable guardian and/or conservator to protect them from future harm.

Other steps to prevent abusive situations might include:

♦ getting the caregiver trained to handle the person's needs

♦ hiring a CNA to provide help with the more strenuous caregiving tasks

♦ providing regular caregiver relief to the primary caregiver by other family members

♦ enrolling the person 3 days a week in an Adult Day Health Care program

♦ sending the person to a respite facility a few days each month

♦ helping the caregiver with stress management

♦ using health care, mental health, or financial POA(s)

Watch for signs of the person abusing the caregiver – biting, hitting, demanding, verbally abusive, or fighting the caregiver.

Reporting Abusive Situations

♦ Determine if the person needs to be removed from a dangerous situation.

♦ Take action to ensure the safety and welfare of the person.

♦ Work with the person, caregiver, and family to immediately stop the neglect, abuse, or exploitation.

> *Report suspected or alleged abuse, neglect, or exploitation to both -- a police officer and your local Adult Protective Services.*

Law enforcement officers can help you remove the adult from a dangerous situation. The officer can make an arrest if they determine a crime was committed. The police report can be used at a later date for criminal and civil court actions.

Every state has Adult Protective Services, which accepts reports of abuse, neglect, and exploitation for vulnerable adults. The APS staff offers resources and information to the older adult, their family members and others when services can benefit the adult. These services can include home delivered meals, home health, or placement in a care setting, but cannot remove the adult from an immediate dangerous situation.

Be prepared to report what happened, when and where it happened, and who the suspected perpetrator might be.

Emotional Health Concerns

Stress

Stress is actually a good thing. What you want is less *distress*. Distress is how you feel when there is either *too much* or *too little* stress in your life. It is important to determine the reasons for the distress and then take quick action to remove the distress.

Are you or your person bored, tired, or unhappy? Try these changes – change your routine, invite visitors to the house or get out with other people every week, go somewhere new, have someone else take your person to lunch once a week, take a class, become a volunteer for a cause you enjoy.

Is your person anxious, irritable, or frustrated? Are you burned-out, exhausted, or over-whelmed? Look for ways to limit the stress in your lives. Plan some enjoyable leisure activities (painting, gardening) and set aside time for them. Let yourself laugh – let yourself cry – both are important. Humor is a powerful antidote to distress. Humor is a great way to relieve tension. Play games. Do something you enjoy each day. Find time to be alone – a time to be quiet. Read a good book, knit, watch a favorite game show.

Be flexible – learn to navigate change. When possible change the world around you. When you cannot change reality, try changing how you view and respond to the reality. If you or your person is loosing your hearing – try purchasing an amplifier for the TV to watch the evening news. If the reporter's voices are still garbled – try reading the morning news paper on the patio after breakfast.

Relationships are important. Keep open and enjoyable communication with your person. Share your feelings. Talk to someone (external) you trust about what is bothering you. Accept support and respite from others. Visit with your neighbors. Call or spend time with family and friends. Join a church.

Signs and Symptoms of Stress

Watch for these signs and symptoms of stress in your person, yourself, and others around you.

- Negative emotions and actions – anxiety, fatigue, frustration, low self esteem, or irritability.
- Subtle warnings – tense shoulder muscles, sweaty palms, chewing on fingernails, or withdrawal.
- Physical ailments – lingering colds, headaches, stomach distress, ulcers, or high blood pressure.

Caregiver Stress

Stress is inherent in caregiving. It is unrealistic that stress can be totally avoided. Pay attention to your responses to caregiving stress. Being frustrated, mad or angry are common feelings of caregivers. If you find yourself arguing or yelling at your person consider these as warning signs. If you find yourself pushing, shaking, or hitting your person – you need help – seek immediate solutions enlisting the help of others.

Take care of yourself. That means – like yourself, enjoy yourself, feel good about yourself, and do things you enjoy. Practice relaxation techniques – deep breathing exercises, muscle relaxation exercises, walking in the fresh air, or even enjoying a nap. Find articles or books about reducing caregiver stress and practice their helpful suggestions.

Caregiver prayer –
"Grant me the serenity to accept things I cannot change,
the courage to change things I can,
and the wisdom to know the difference...
and please grant me a sense of humor."

Loss and Grieving

Experiencing losses is a normal part of aging experience. Deaths of close friends and family are not the only losses experienced by seniors. Loss of productivity, loss of income, loss of control, loss of importance, loss of independence, and physical losses such as dancing, balance, hearing, sight, or even losing their teeth – acknowledge the losses of your person.

In coping with loss, it is natural and normal to experience feelings of grief, sadness, loneliness, despair, helplessness, powerlessness, and depression. Part of the human experience is to have these reactive feelings to a loss. The grieving process may take weeks and even months for your person to resolve.

During the early stages your person may eat and sleep too much or not enough. They could have difficulty with concentration, attention-span, memory, and withdrawal from doing pleasurable activities.

Although these are normal responses – it becomes a serious problem when these symptoms do not diminish over a few months and continue to interfere with your person's daily functioning. Should these responses and feelings persist seek advice from your person's doctor.

Depression

Depression is a serious medical illness. It is a mood disorder in which feelings of sadness, loss, anger, or frustration interfere with everyday life for more than a few weeks. Depression can be a sign of a medical problem or illness. Depression is also a side effect of many drugs commonly prescribed for the elderly.

A number of factors can play their parts in depression. They can include alcohol or drug abuse, life events such as loss of a spouse or social isolation, medical conditions such as a major illness or chronic pain, medications, or sleeping problems.

If you suspect that your person has depression consult your doctor.

After medical problems, illnesses, or medication side effects are ruled out by your person's doctor, depression can be effectively treated with antidepressants, talk therapy, and the improvement of their psychosocial environments.

As your person's caregiver, you can provide positive responses when talking to your person. Frequently offer support using encouraging sentences – *I care about what is happening to you. You are not alone. You are not crazy. I am sorry you are in so much pain. What can I do to help?*

Signs and Symptoms of Depression

- Constant pervasive sadness – lives in a gray world
- Difficulty concentrating/ decisions
- Loss of interest – hobbies, friends, activities
- Change in sleep habits – too little or too much
- Sudden weight loss or gain
- Increases in drinking alcohol or in using drugs or tobacco
- Statements of death or suicide – *"You are better off without me", "I see no reason to live", or "I'd be better off dead".*

Infection and Infection Control

Chain of Infection

Pathogenic micro-organisms or ***germs*** are the cause of an infection. Bacteria, virus, fungus (molds or yeast), and parasite are all examples of germs. Germs are found everywhere. Germs cause no harmful effect to healthy people.

Common bacterial infections include urinary track or blood infections, certain types of pneumonia, and infected sores or wounds. Food poisoning is often caused by E-coli, salmonella, or staphylococcal bacteria. Tuberculosis in the lungs is a bacterial infection.

Common viral infections include influenza, Hepatitis A, B, or C, and AIDS or HIV. The Herpes zoster virus causes chicken pox and shingles. Shingles occurs most commonly in people over the age of 60.

Germs grow or multiply in conditions of oxygen or air, moisture, darkness, temperature, and nourishment. Germs that cause infections are like reservoirs. Sick people, contaminated food, dirty hands, unclean bathrooms, and even doorknobs are the source of these reservoirs of germs.

Germs exit their source in many ways. Germs leave people or animals from the respiratory track, gastrointestinal track, genitourinary track (reproductive or urinary), skin, mucous membranes (eyes or mouth), or blood. Germs on non-living items live on the surface of objects or linens or in the food.

The germ moves from the source of the infection in many ways:

> **Direct contact** – such as a hand touching the infected person or touching bowel movement, blood or other infected body fluids.

> **Indirect contact** – a sick person drinks from a glass, and then a well person drinks from same glass. Other examples are touching a wound dressing, soiled bed linens, or contaminated item.

Droplet – a sneeze, cough, or talking within 3 feet of the sick person.

Airborne – carried by droplet or dust particle for example from a person with influenza, chicken pox, or tuberculosis.

Contaminated food or water is ingested.

If you do not have a tissue -- cough or sneeze into your elbow.

Germs enter their new host in similar ways as they exit their source. For example, germs can enter a human via the lungs, mouth, skin, eyes, nose, or blood. Germs can also be contaminated onto bed linens, door knobs, and food.

Coughing or sneezing helps the body defend itself from infections; so are tears in the eyes, mucous membranes in the nose and throat, and cilia in the lungs. Fever, inflammation, and immune responses are internal defenses. Gastric acid in your stomach acts as a barrier against germs to prevent infections.

The last link of the chain of infection is the susceptible host. The elderly are more at risk to infection due many reasons – stress, chronic disease, poor nutritional status, inadequate hydration, medications, poor hygiene, open breaks or wounds in their skin, weakness, or depressed immune systems – just to name the most common. In the elderly, simple infections can develop into serious complications.

Signs and symptoms of infection

People with infections might have some of these symptoms:
- A fever, chills, or a sub-normal temperature
- A cough, sore throat, runny or stuffy nose
- Pain, muscle or body aches, headaches, restlessness, tiredness, or fatigue
- Swelling, heat or redness, pus or drainage near a wound
- Diarrhea or cramps -- Nausea or vomiting
- Weight loss, lethargy, or abnormally low blood pressure

> *If you think your person might have an infection –*
> *consult your doctor.*

Seek urgent medical care if you observe any of these warning signs in your sick person:

- Difficulty breathing or shortness of breath
- Pain or pressure in the chest of abdomen
- Sudden dizziness
- Confusion
- Severe or persistent vomiting
- Frequent and/or painful urination, cloudy, bloody, or smelly urine, or back pain

Infection Control

It is important for you as a caregiver to continually prevent the spreading of infection – by breaking the chain of infection. Guidelines for standard precautions for Infection Control include:

- Hand washing
- Using personal protective items like gloves or masks
- Handling and disinfection of contaminated items or surfaces
- Disposal of sharp objects carefully in a proper container

> *Wash your hands often*

The single best way to prevent the spread of infection is frequent hand washing. Hands must be washed after coughing, sneezing, or blowing your nose – after smoking – after using the bathroom. Wash your hands before caring for your person – preparing food – helping with activities of daily living – before and after using latex gloves.

Typically you do not need to wear latex gloves or a mask in the home setting. But you may want to consider using them if you are helping your person with toileting tasks. The practice of using personal protective items is discussed in *Personal Care*, as is the handling of soiled linens or clothing.

Germs can be transferred from your hands to almost any item. Germs can survive for several hours on most surfaces. Practice a routine of daily disinfecting household surfaces. Using a spray bottle, prepare a solution of 1 part bleach to 10 parts water. Use gloves to protect you hands from the bleach. Start with a clean cloth, spray the solution on the cloth and walk around the house wiping off door knobs, counter tops, grab bars, wheelchair handles, or light switchers. Rinse the cloth often and spray additional solution as needed. When cleaning up a contaminated floor, soak the mop in a bleach solution to kill germs.

When using sharp objects such as lancets used for blood sugar checks, medication needles, or disposable razors handle them carefully. Only use a needle or lancet one time. Place the protective plastic covering back over the needle. Dispose all sharp objects into a closable puncture-resistant container (like a large, clean, used coffee can). Store this container in a safe place. When it becomes full, you can throw it out in your outside trash.

Food Preparation and Storage

Wash your hands often

In *Supervisory Care*, you read about the importance of nutrition. In the last section you read about germs, infections, and infection control. This section combines cooking and infection control to help you to avoid causing a food-borne illness. A food-borne illness is a disease that is carried or transmitted to people by food. Food-borne illness is caused by eating foods that have become contaminated by bacteria, viruses, fungus, parasites, or even chemicals.

It is important to keep the kitchen, food preparation, or dining areas of the house clean and sanitary. It is important to apply infection control practices when you are touching food. It is even more important to properly store or prepare the foods to keep everyone from getting sick from the foods you prepare.

Your person may be more at risk to a food-borne illness. Their immune systems and resistance may be weakened with frailty, illness, chronic diseases, or medications. There are many symptoms related to food-borne illnesses. Nausea, vomiting, and diarrhea are the most common. Other symptoms such as cramps, headaches, muscle aches, fever and chills also occur.

Time-temperature Control Avoid allowing food to remain too long at temperatures in the danger zone. Promptly place cold or frozen food directly in the refrigerator or freezer after purchase. Refrigerated or cooked foods should not be allowed to sit-out at room temperature for more than the length of the meal.

Store serve, or heat all foods at the correct temperatures – cold food cold and cooked food hot. If you prepare food ahead, then store the prepared food in the refrigerator or freezer.

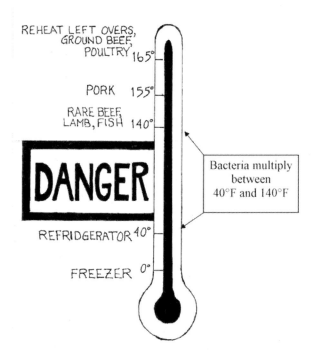

REHEAT LEFT OVERS, GROUND BEEF, POULTRY 165°

PORK 155°

RARE BEEF, LAMB, FISH 140°

DANGER

Bacteria multiply between 40°F and 140°F

REFRIDGERATOR 40°

FREEZER 0°

Place a functioning thermometer in every refrigerator or freezer.

Maintain your refrigerator at a temperature of 40°F or below. Maintain your freezer at a temperature of 0°F or below.

Almost any food made from animal products, such as meat, fish, poultry, eggs, and dairy products are considered to be potentially hazardous foods. Refried beans, cooked rice, and baked potatoes are also examples of potentially hazardous foods. These types of foods contain *protein and moisture* that germs need to grow and multiply.

Keep all potentially hazardous foods refrigerated. Cook or reheat foods to the temperatures that kill germs. These foods, except for eggs and dairy products should be cooked to heat all parts of the food to a temperature of at least 140°F.

The following table indicates which foods should be cooked to a hotter internal temperature.

Food type:	At least
Ground beef and poultry	165°F
Poultry stuffing, stuffed meats, and stuffing containing meat	165°F
Pork or any food containing pork	155°F
Rare roast beef – internal temperature, lamb, fish, and seafood	140°F
Rare steak – internal temperature	130°F
Leftovers are reheated to	165°F

Check foods left unrefrigerated, such as fruits or breads for spoilage or mold. If you think food is not safe to eat – such as it smells bad, the un-opened can is swollen, moldy food, tainted meats, or spoiled fish – throw it out.

If in doubt – throw it out.

Cross-contamination Foods can become contaminated in many ways. The most common is when disease-causing germs (or micro-organisms) are present in food or on preparation surfaces. Cross-contamination occurs when germs are transmitted from one surface or food to another food. Your hands, knives, cutting boards, or cooking utensils can also cross-contaminate foods.

Keep raw food separated from cooked food.

Follow these practices. Be very careful when working with raw meats. Store or thaw them on the bottom shelf of the refrigerator. Keep all foods stored in refrigerator in covered containers or sealed bags. Use separate bowls, pans, cutting boards, or utensils for raw and uncooked foods. For example, if you are grilling hamburgers – use one plate to take them to the grill and a clean plate to take them to the table.

Cook raw meats or any food you add potentially hazardous food to the correct temperatures to kill any germs. Follow the chart for these temperatures. Wash your hands after handling raw meat, fish, or poultry.

Wash raw fruits and raw vegetables in water to remove soil and other contaminates before cutting them or combining them with other ingredients which are being cooked or served. Store room temperature foods in clean, dry locations like on shelves or in the pantry. Use covered containers.

Do not use sponges in the kitchen. Change your dish clothes often.

Start and finish with a clean and sanitized kitchen. Hand wash dishes and cooking items using hot, sudsy water and rinsing with hot water. Use a drying rack and air dry dishes. If you use the dishwasher, use the heat drying cycle. After cleaning them with sudsy water, sanitize the counter tops, stove surface, microwave oven, oven door, refrigerator, and sinks using about 2 gallons of cool water in the sink with 4 tablespoons of chlorine bleach. You can soak your plastic cutting boards in this solution for a few minutes and then rinsing them with hot water. Do not forget to put a fresh bag in the covered garbage container and place the full garbage bag and recyclables in their outside containers.

Personal Hygiene Bacteria grow well on skin. Your hands are always contaminated with bacteria. Proper hand washing prevents food-borne disease. Wash your hands after going to the bathroom, smoking, before preparing food, and after handling unclean objects or raw meats. If you taste the food, use a utensil not your hand. Do not lick your fingers, touch your face, or hair during food preparation.

Keep your fingernails short and clean. Remove hand jewelry prior to preparing food. If you have a cut, burn, or wound on your hand be sure you have it covered with a clean bandage.

Cough or sneeze into your elbow – not your hands. Wash your hands after using a tissue. If you have a bad cold, flu, diarrhea, vomiting, or sore throat find someone else to prepare the food, until you are feeling better.

Creating Menus and Grocery Lists

Creating a 2-3 week cycle of menus eases some of the stress of being caregiver *and* chef – especially if both caregiving and cooking tasks are new to you. The *Nutrition* section in *Supervisory Care* discusses warning signs of poor nutrition, the basic food groups, making good nutritional choices, and the importance of serving 3 meals and 2 snacks each day.

A written menu helps:

- Provide a variety of meals – avoids serving chicken three days in a row
- Prepare and serve your person's favorite foods
- Balance basic food groups through-out the day
- Plan light cooking days and cook-ahead days
- Freeze and serve leftovers to avoid wasting food
- Make creating a grocery list easier
- Save money – buying only the food you plan to use

Creating the 2-3 week cycle of menus can be a fun activity with you and your person – or you can ask a family member jot down you and your person's ideas and create the first cycle for you. Try repeating the cycle for a couple of times – writing in changes, new ideas, or dislikes. Create a new copy of the menus and slip them into a clear page saver and keep them handy for reference.

The sample menu for a two week cycle gives you some ideas. Notice that some meals are planned as eating with others, eating out, ordering meals delivered, and using leftovers.

Keep take-out menus from local restaurants that deliver handy.

Be flexible in switching days – and substituting pork chops for ham slice if pork chops are on sale. You can serve the larger meal at noon and simplify the evening meal with lighter lunch-like foods.

The menus give you a general plan – you can be creative – cooking a chicken dish from a favorite recipe. You can also choose to heat and serve a purchased frozen entree. The goal is to provide a balanced diet (grains, proteins, dairy, vegetables, and fruits), variety of foods, and not *burnout* the chef.

Encourage your person to share the task of preparing meals.

Grocery Lists

When you make a grocery list let your fingers do the walking. The following list shows the sections of the store and most foods from the first week menu found on the following page. Start shopping in the non-perishable food isles first, do the produce area, the refrigerated and frozen foods, saving the bakery for last (these foods smash). Keep a running list of items that need replacing – like tissues or laundry detergent.

Keep cold and frozen foods in their temperature zones.

Groceries	— 2 boxes of breakfast cereal — oatmeal — crackers — cookies — microwave pop-corn, — bag of chips — 2 cans of fruit — 2 cans of vegetables, —cranberry juice, — tomato soup — vegetable soup — 1 can tuna — 1 can chicken, — 2 boxes of tissues — laundry detergent, bleach
Produce	— 6 apples — 4 bananas — cantaloupe — cucumber — bell pepper — 2 heads lettuce — tomatoes —medium sweet potato —celery — carrots
Meats	— cube steak — ½ lb lean ground beef — a ham slice
Deli	— ¼ lb sliced turkey - ½ lb coleslaw - sliced cheese -string cheese- bacon
Dairy	— 1 gallon low fat milk — low fat creamer — cottage cheese — 6 yogurts — a dozen large eggs
Frozen foods	— 2 chicken/pasta dinners — 2 Mexican dinner entrees — bag of broccoli — pre-cooked breakfast sausage — fish sticks— French fries — ice cream
Bakery	— coffee cake — bread — small rolls — cookies — fruit pie

Quite a list! If your person is very independent an outing to buy groceries can count as her exercise for the day. If your person is unable to walk this far – consider having them use the motorized shopping cart. Selecting items at the store offers a useful activity of decision making and choice.

	Week 1 Monday	Week 1 Tuesday	Week 1 Wednesday	Week 1 Thursday	Week 1 Friday	Week 1 Saturday	Week 1 Sunday
Breakfast	Cold cereal, fruit	Boiled eggs, toast, bacon	Hot cereal, fruit	Scrambled eggs, toast, juice	Cold cereal, fruit	Waffles, sausage cantaloupe	Coffee cake cantaloupe
Noon Meal	Grilled cheese sandwich tomato soup, veggies	Tuna salad on lettuce, roll	Turkey sand-wich lettuce tomato	Hamburger, lettuce tomato, chips	Chicken salad on lettuce, roll	PBJ sandwich vegetable soup	Large meal with family
Evening Meal	Chicken Pasta dish broccoli garden salad	Cube steak Green vegetable Sliced tomatoes	Ham slice Sweet potato Cottage cheese	Mexican frozen entree – with rice and beans	Fish sticks Coleslaw French fries	Order pizza delivery veggie sticks	Leftover pizza Garden salad
Snacks	apple; yogurt	½ banana; cookies	apple; ice cream	veggies; yogurt	string cheese; pie	celery; ice cream	ice cream or pie

	Week 2 Monday	Week 2 Tuesday	Week 2 Wednesday	Week 2 Thursday	Week 2 Friday	Week 2 Saturday	Week 2 Sunday
Breakfast	Cold cereal, fruit	Fried eggs, toast cantaloupe	Hot cereal, fruit	Spinach, ham, & cheese quiche, toast	Cold cereal, fruit	Pancakes, bacon	Hot cereal, fruit
Noon Meal	Cottage cheese, fruit crackers	Chicken nuggets, Chips, apple sauce	Turkey hot dog, bun, baked beans	Turkey sandwich creamed soup	Leftover quiche Garden salad, roll	Sloppy Joes Veggie sticks	Brunch out
Evening Meal	Sunday's leftovers from family meal	Cabbage rolls, Whipped Potatoes, mixed veggies	Beef stroganoff Garden salad Roll	Tacos – beef, lettuce, tomatoes, graded cheese	Baked haddock Scalloped potatoes Green beans	Go to Chinese restaurant tonight	Leftover Chinese, rice, egg rolls
Snacks	veggies; cookies	PB/celery stick; pie	½ banana; ice cream	apple; yogurt	cheese; pop corn	apple; ice cream	cookies; ice cream

The House They Live In

> This chapter addresses the physical environment where the person requiring care lives or visits. As you read each topic, take a moment to walk through the apartment or house. Look at each area from the perspective of safety. Consider both your needs as a caregiver and the special needs of the person you are caring for.

Safety in Every Room

Walk through all rooms in the home. While standing in any room or area, ask yourself the questions from the checklist. Make notes and implement safety changes as needed.

Bedroom Safety

The bed should be accessible from both sides. Ensure the walkway between the bed and the bathroom is not obstructed with other furniture. Consider placing night lights by the bed, in the hall, and in the bathroom.

A good night's rest requires a comfortable bed. Check the bed for comfort. Is it firm and in good condition? Replace a soft, saggy, or soiled mattress. If needed, invest in a water proof mattress cover keep to keep the mattress dry. Use a thick mattress pad to increase softness. Are the sheets clean? Are there several comfortable pillows? Is the blanket or comforter the right thickness for the season? Is there a spare blanket?

Is there a night stand or bedside table? Use this area for storing glasses, hearing aides, and/or dentures at night. Is there a bedside lamp? This lamp can be bright enough for reading in bed or available for middle of the night use if needed. If there is a TV in the room, is the remote convenient to the bed or bedroom recliner?

Home Safety Checklist

♦ Is the furniture in the room easy to walk around?

♦ Is the furniture in the room appropriate? Avoid chairs that roll.   Consider dining chairs with arms to provide support for sitting and standing-up.

♦ Is the room cluttered?

♦ Are the obstacles the might cause a person to trip or fall?   Such as a throw rug, a torn carpet — lamp, appliance, electrical, or phone chords running across the floor?

♦ Are the walking surfaces smooth?

♦ If there are stairs, are there hand railings? Are all hand railings in good repair?

♦ If needed, are there hallway railings?

♦ Does the room have both natural light (from a window or door) and working electrical lights to assure safety?

♦ When a wheelchair is needed -- are the doorways wide enough to accommodate a wheelchair?   Is there a ramp at entrance doors?   Are floors – tile or hardwood (not shag carpet) for safe rolling?   Furniture easy to navigate around?

♦ Are there working furnace and air conditioning units with adjustable wall controls to keep the room temperatures between 68°F and 85°F at all times?

♦ Is furniture placed to avoid air conditioning, ceiling fan, or open window drafts?

♦ Does plumbing work?   Cold and hot water?   Hot water heater set below 120°F?

♦ Does the bathroom have grab bars?

♦ Is the garbage stored in covered containers lined with plastic bags?

♦ Are there any tell-tail signs of insects or rodents?

♦ Is the home clean, in good repair, and free of odors?

NOTES:

Place a straight backed chair convenient for your person sit on while they are putting on their clothing or their socks and shoes. Neat dresser drawers and closets make dressing a pleasure. Keep the room uncluttered.

As mentioned in *Personal Care*, if a hospital bed is used – do not use the side rails. The risk of injury, entrapment, or accidental death due to the use of side rails a serious safety issue. If your person has dementia, s/he might try to climb over the rail. If your person is frail or paralyzed, then s/he might not have the strength to free themselves from between the side rail and the bed.

Do not use side rails on beds.

If your person tends to roll side-to-side in the bed, consider placing the box-spring and/or mattress directly on the floor. For extra cushion, place a skid-resistant fluffy rug beside the bed. If your person tries to get out of bed alone, consider other options, such as motion sensors, night-time toileting schedule, full-length body pillows, or special lower-height beds.

Ask your doctor about adequate night-time pain control.

Bathroom Safety

There are many levels of safety in the bathroom. To start with, a supply of toilet paper, soap, wash cloths, towels should be accessible.

Like any other room, the bathroom should have adequate light, smooth and uncluttered floors, no rugs to trip on, and uncluttered counter surfaces. Medications should be in cabinets if stored in the bathroom. Cleaning chemicals, toxics, and poisons should not be stored in the bathroom.

Soiled linen and soiled clothing should be stored in closed containers. Garbage should be kept in a covered container lined with plastic bags. The room should be kept clean and free of odors.

The linen closet is a handy place to store first aid supplies. Keep the supplies in a kit or basket that can be quickly and easily moved to any place in the home.

Review the following checklist to enhance bathroom usability and safety.

- Is there a supply of cold and hot water available?
- Is the hot water temperature maintained between 95°F and 120°F?
- Shower floor and/or tub bottom should be skid-resistant?
- Install grab bars on the walls of the shower and/or tub.
- Use a shower chair and install a shower handheld hose.
- Is there a fan or window in the toilet area?
- Install a raised toilet seat.
- Install a call bell (remote doorbell from Radio Shack).
- Install grab bars on the walls of the toilet.

Chemicals – toxic or poisonous – combustible or flammable

Cleaning products and poisonous or toxic materials should be stored in a safe or locked area away from food preparation and storage areas, dining areas, or where medications storage areas. Consider putting these items in a locked cabinet or high shelf in the laundry room.

Combustible or flammable liquids and other hazardous materials such a weed killers, garden products, or automotive products should be stored in a locked cabinet or high shelf in the garage or a locked outside storage shed.

Keep all products in their original labeled containers. Read the back of the label. Read and follow all product usage instructions, directions, cautions, hazards, or warnings. A poison has instructions which include calling a doctor or a Poison Control Center. If the label includes the words **"KEEP OUT OF REACH OF CHILDREN"**, consider it toxic.

Locks

Install locks on cabinets used to store medications or chemicals. Sometimes *baby locks* (small plastic locks) are enough to keep drawers or cabinet doors closed. These are easiest to install. Key locks must be drilled. Newer locks can be screwed to the inside of the doors and shelf – then released using a *magnet*-type key. These locks can not be seen from the outside – but the door does not open when locked.

All doors exiting to the outside should have a quality working deadbolt lock for safety. Consider putting in a *peep hole* in the front doors. Consider giving a key to a trusted neighbor or family member – who can let you in if you lock yourself out – or can get into the house if you call them for help.

Doors with locks inside the house should have keys or *oyster-can* openers kept in a permanent location outside the door – in case your person locks the door and can't get to the door to open it. Consider replacing inside doors with non-locking knobs.

If you do not want your person with dementia – silently leaving the house – install *door/window alarms*. They indicate with either words (*"back door opened"*) or make audible sounds (ringing, chiming, alarm) when the door or window is opened.

Pets

Before reading further – discuss these questions with your person:

- ◆ Is this pet a hazard to your person?
- ◆ Does the pet bite?
- ◆ Does the pet jump on your person?
- ◆ Could the pet make your person fall?
- ◆ Is your person allergic to the pet?

This is a good example where you as the caregiver must balance the pet hazard with your person's dignity, independence, self-determination, and choice. *Loosing a pet can be as hard as loosing a loved person.*

You can take the appropriate adoption steps if *everyone* agrees the pet is a safety or health hazard to your person. Perhaps a family member or close neighbor can adopt the pet and bring it back for visits. You can also look on-line for many pet rescue groups if you need to find the pet a new home.

If the pet stays – "pets" for the purpose of this topic are defined as dogs, cats, birds, reptiles, and fish. Any other animal safety issues are left to the reader's discretion. Any dog or cat in the home should be licensed/tagged consistent with local ordinances. For dogs and cats, during regular check-ups with your local vet discuss your person's needs. Require your vet to keep the pet current with required shots – especially those vaccinations (such as rabies), which keep your person safe. Keep the pet groomed – including keeping the nails/claws short and dull.

Ensure the pet's habitat (fish bowl, aquarium, bird cage, kennel, rug, or bed) is kept free from algae, insects, and other particulate matter. Keep the habitat clean to avoid odors from rotting food or excess pet wastes. This includes cleaning up the pet waste in the litter box, fish bowl, aquarium, bird cage, home, or outdoor area.

As the caregiver, when your person is not able, ensure that the pet remains safe and cared for and that your person is not harmed by the pet.

Do not keep or allow the pet in the same room where food is prepared to eat.

If your person is suddenly absent from the home, arrange temporary lodging or kenneling for the pet.

Deal with this matter at a later date.

Safety Outdoors

Don't forget to take a walk outdoors. Is there a covered patio area? Shade is a requirement for sensitive, older skin. Provide an outdoor table and chairs for relaxation. Is there a flat smooth walking area or path into the yard? If needed, is the patio and yard accessible to a wheelchair? Also look to see:

- Is the outdoor area clean and odor free?

- Is it insect, rodent, and hazard free?

- Yard tools or outdoor chemicals, toxins, or poisons should not be stored in this outdoor area. Keep/lock outdoor hazards in the garage.

- If there is a shed in the yard, is it locked?

- Is the yard maintained? Is the fence in good repair?

Does your person live in a winter climate with snow and icy conditions? Arrange for all outside walks to be cleared after storms. Put salt or kitty litter on your person's icy areas.

Outdoor Water Safety

Swimming pools or other bodies of water are a serious safety hazard for many different reasons. Is the water fresh, clean and debris free? Is there a hand railing on the steps into the pool? Is the swimming pool, spa, or outdoor water feature in good working order?

Is this unfenced body of water a hazard to your person? If you have *any concerns*, **never leave your person outdoors by themselves unattended.** Consider installing a lock on any door or window leading into the pool/spa area. Consider putting a permanent pool-safety fence around the pool/spa area. These fences have self-closing, self-latching, and lockable gates. If a pool-safety fence is used, keep it locked.

If you are a caregiver in a home with a swimming pool – learn CPR.

Fire Safety

Walk through all rooms in the home. While standing in any room or area, locate the closest exit to the room and the house. Note windows that might be used as possible emergency escape routes. Check to see if these windows open easily.

In an older home, install battery operated smoke detectors according to the manufacture's instructions. Hardware and home improvement stores sell battery operated smoke detectors. A newer home might have hard-wired smoke detectors.

Look for or install smoke detectors in:

- ♦ every bedroom,
- ♦ hallways that lead from bedrooms,
- ♦ hallways or rooms adjacent to the kitchen,
- ♦ storage rooms or laundry rooms,
- ♦ and/or attached garages

Learn how to test smoke alarms to verify they are working properly. Check them once a month. Change batteries as needed or at least once a year.

Locate or install a small portable, all-purpose fire extinguisher with a 2A-10-BC rating. This type of fire extinguisher puts out **all types** of residential fires. Depending upon the size of the house, consider having two extinguishers. One located in or near the kitchen and another located near bedrooms or laundry room. Learn how to operate the fire extinguisher and replace it as recommended by the manufacture.

Once a month -- test smoke alarms and check fire extinguishers – review escape routes

Are all phones labeled with a "9-1-1" sticker?

Preventing Fires

Have the heating system inspected at the beginning of each heating season. Use fire places or portable space heaters with extreme caution. Keep anything that will burn at least three feet away.

Older homes can have serious wiring problems, ranging from old appliances with bad wiring, faulty wiring, or overloaded electrical circuits. Have electrical work done by an electrician.

Cooking safety

Be cautious when cooking. Keep anything that can catch fire, such as pot holders, towels, plastics and clothing away from the stove. Keep the stove area clean and free of grease. Discard grease in a closed glass jar directly into the outside trash can.

Stay in the kitchen when frying, grilling, or broiling. If you need to leave the kitchen, turn off the stove. Stay in the home when simmering, baking, roasting, or boiling food. Check the food regularly and use a timer to remind you the food is cooking.

Smoking

Determine if your person is safe to smoke unsupervised. If necessary, keep all smoking materials in a locked cabinet. Ask your person to consider only smoking outside in a covered patio area. The unsafe use of smoking materials – cigarettes, cigars, pipes, matches, ashtrays – is the leading cause of fire deaths among aging adults. If your person smokes – encourage them to quit.

When there is smoking in the home – use extreme caution. Smoke sitting up – preferably at a table away from upholstered furniture. Never smoke in bed or when you are tired. Provide a large, noncombustible ashtray. Empty the ashtray into a toilet or metal container in the evening.

Oxygen

Oxygen is ordered by a doctor when a person has breathing difficulties. Oxygenators are machines that convert air into pure oxygen. Oxygen bottles have valves that release oxygen at various levels. Oxygen bottles should be securely attached in an upright position to the back of a wheelchair or in a supplied bottle/canister holder with wheels.

Ask the oxygen supply company train you or your person with the system they provide.

Frequently inspect the tubing from the machine or bottle that goes on your person's nose of the user. Keep the nose piece clean. If tubing is longer and lays on the floor – ensure that it does not become bent or twisted. Use care when walking with tubing on the floor to avoid tripping.

Special safety rules apply when oxygen is being used in the home. A sign on the front door of the house should warn visitors that oxygen is used in the home. No open flames should be allowed in a home where oxygen is used. This includes candles, gas or wood burning fire places, matches, cigarette lighters, or lit cigarettes. Smoking should never be allowed in the same room.

Spare oxygen canisters or bottles should be stored in an upright position secured to a wall or placed in a custom storage box. Empty bottles should be stored separately in an upright position.

In Case of Fire

Develop a fire escape plan. Locate escape routes for each room. Review these routes with your person while in that room. Note windows that might be used as possible emergency escape routes. If the room is not on a ground floor, locate inside or outside stairways. Practice your plan twice a year.

Evacuating the Home

In case of fire – **stay calm**. What escape routes lead away from the fire or smoke? Get your person to safety, away from both the fire and the smoke as quickly as possible. Smoke inhalation into a person's lungs can be deadly.

When there are flames or smoke:

+ Do not attempt to put the fire out.

+ If you get caught in smoke, get down and crawl low under the smoke.

+ Do not stop to call the fire department.

+ Do not stop to collect belongings.

+ Call 9-1-1 from your meeting place outside the home.

+ Do not return to the burning building.

+ Alert the firemen if your loved one is still in the home.

If your person is non-ambulatory or physically challenged, s/he can be placed on a sturdy blanket and pulled or dragged out of the home.

If clothing catches on fire have your person **STOP, DROP, AND ROLL**. If your person is in a wheelchair or bed and catches on fire, use water, a heavy blanket, or wet towel to smother the flames.

At night, if you hear the smoke alarm and if the closed door or door knob to the bedroom is warm, then use your second way out of the room. If smoke, heat, or flames block your exit routes, stay in the room with the doors closed. Place a wet towel under to door and call 9-1-1.

Tell the person on the phone the location of your room within the home. Is it in the back or front of the home? Is it on the second floor?

When to Fight the Fire

You should only fight a fire with a fire extinguisher when all the following items are **true**:

- Everyone has left or is leaving the building.

- The fire department has been called.

- The fire is small and confined to the immediate areas where it started, such as in a wastebasket, cushion, small appliance, stove, etc.

- You can fight the fire with your back to a safe escape route.

- Your extinguisher has a 2A-10-BC rating and is in good working order.

- You have had training in use of the extinguisher and are confident you can operate it effectively.

If you have the *slightest doubt* about whether or not to fight the fire – *don't*. Instead get out, closing the door behind you to slow the spread of the fire. Let the professionals do their job.

Using a Fire Extinguisher

Remember the word **PASS** when using a fire extinguisher:

- **Pull** the pin and hold the extinguisher with the nozzle pointing away from you. Some units have the releasing of a lock or latch or pressing the puncture lever.

- **Aim low.** Point the extinguisher at the base of the fire.

- **Squeeze** or press the lever slowly and evenly.

- **Sweep** the nozzle from side to side until the fire goes out.

Shut off the extinguisher and then watch carefully for a rekindling of the fire.

When there is an Emergency

Action is needed in the event of an emergency in the home. An emergency can be a medical emergency, a fall or other accident in the home. There can be a fire in the home. Emergency response techniques include calling 9-1-1 or calling the doctor or a family member, responding to the medical emergency or accident before help arrives. Evacuating the home if there is a fire.

First aid kit

Be prepared for minor emergencies by having a first aid kit. Keep a purchased first aid kit or first aid supplies in a basket on a shelf in the linen closet. The kit or basket can be quickly and easily moved to any place in the home when needed.

First aid supplies might include various sizes of band aids, sterile bandages or gauze pads, antiseptic wipes, tweezers, scissors, tape, hand sanitizer, and disposable latex gloves.

Training for Basic First Aid and CPR

A **basic first aid class** covers topics like recognizing life-threatening and nonlife-threatening conditions on a conscious or unconscious person. It demonstrates first aid procedures – such as stopping bleeding or responding to a seizure. A **CPR (Cardio Pulmonary Resuscitation)** class covers topics like checking for a pulse, clearing an airway, back blows, abdominal thrusts, rescue breathing, and performing CPR.

Learn Basic First Aid and CPR.

The *American Red Cross* and the *American Heart Association* offer community classes to train you or other caregivers in basic first aid or CPR. You bring home laminated skill cards and student workbooks to keep as references. Taking a class can help you save the life of your person if there is an emergency.

Seniors Living Alone

If your person lives alone – independently – discuss and practice how they can react to an emergency when they are home alone. Provide a cordless phone that they can carry with them inside the home. Have them place the phone by the bed at night.

Label all phones with a "9-1-1" sticker

Other ideas include getting your person a cell phone or a *call button* service. Program phones and teach your person how to quickly dial emergency contacts like yourself, their closest neighbor, their doctors, or the local fire department. Consider a home monitoring system service. This type of service can use the cell phone or will provide a bracelet or necklace call button device that allows a remote operator to contact the person or sends help to the home – when your person presses the button.

The Call for Help

When your person is in distress & you decide to call 9-1-1 for help:

- Tell the phone number from which you are calling.
- Tell the address and any specific description of how to get to your location.
- Describe the emergency and your person's condition the best you can.

    Is your person:
    - ➢ having difficulty breathing…
    - ➢ fallen and might have possible broken bones…
    - ➢ having a seizure, stroke or heart attack…
    - ➢ bleeding or burned...
- Tell your name and your person's name and their age.
- **Do not hang up.** Answer any questions of the emergency operator. Follow instructions of the emergency operator. Give the phone to another person, if you need to help your person.

When help arrives

Inform the emergency responders about what happened. Remain calm. Give them the **Emergency – Paramedic Sheet**. As discussed in Chapter 5, this sheet contains your person's identification, diagnosis and medical conditions, emergency contact information and has a current medication chart attached. These documents should accompany your person if they are taken to the hospital in an ambulance.

After help arrives call other emergency contacts to notify them of the emergency.

> *Post a copy of the Contact Information Sheet of phone numbers next to your phone.*

Medical Emergencies or Accidents

When your person is in distress, *before help arrives* be prepared to take the following actions.

♦ Remain calm and reassure your person that help is coming.

♦ Monitor your person's airway, breathing, and pulse.

♦ Help your person to rest in the most comfortable position – get a pillow for their head.

♦ Prevent your person for getting chilled or overheated – supply a covering or shade.

♦ Do not give your person anything to drink or eat.

Frequently review the following tables to become familiar with possible symptoms or warning signs.

Emergency	Warning signs / symptoms	Tips – *before help arrives*
Choking *A choking person can die in 4 minutes*	if person is coughing	Encourage them to cough-up the blockage.
	cannot breath, speak, or cough	Try back blows between shoulder blades.
	turns blue collapses	**Refer to your first aid training card.** Begin abdominal thrusts.
Diabetic *Hypoglycemia* Can progress to Insulin Shock	shaking, fast heartbeat faintness, dizzy, fatigue headache, blurred vision sweating hunger	Onset is sudden. Offer ½ cup of orange juice or milk. Test and record blood sugar (below 70mg/dL).
Diabetic *Hyperglycemia* Can progress to Diabetic Coma	extreme thirst frequent urination extreme hunger nausea, abdominal pain drowsiness blurred vision	Onset is gradual. Test and record blood sugar (above 250mg/dL). Follow your person's doctor order concerning diabetic medications.
Difficulty Breathing	Hyperventilation	Have person breath slower, use reassurances.
	Acute Asthma Labored, rapid breathing shortness of breath	Have your person relax, remain sitting Use asthma inhalers as instructed.
Fainting	paleness, dizziness cold / clammy skin blurred vision nausea	Have your person sit/lay down to avoid falling. If fainted– shake person– try to awaken person. Check for signs of breathing and pulse. If fallen– check for injury.
	with Vomiting	Roll your person on her side or turn her head. If needed, wipe out her mouth. Tilt her chin up to keep her air way open

Emergency	Warning signs / symptoms	Tips – *before help arrives*
<u>Unconscious</u>		Shake person – try to awaken person. Check for signs of breathing. **Refer to your CPR training card.**
	<u>and not Breathing</u>	Roll person on their back – clear airway. **Begin rescue breathing.** Check for a pulse.
	<u>with out a Pulse</u>	**Begin CPR.**
<u>Heart Attack</u>	severe squeezing pains in the chest pain radiates from chest to left arm or neck pain across the shoulders to the neck sweating or weakness breathing slows /stops heart slows or stops	**Refer to your CPR training card.** Check for breathing – if your person is not breathing. **Begin rescue breathing.** Check for a pulse. If you can not find a pulse. **Begin CPR** If possible – switch with another person every few minutes. Performing CPR is physically demanding.
<u>Seizures</u>	limbs jerk violently eyes may roll upward breathing may be heavy breathing may stop	Help your person to lie down to avoid injury. Do not restrain your person during the seizure. Do not put *anything* in their mouth.
		<u>After the seizure:</u> Check for breathing. Follow their doctor's instructions if you have been trained to respond to seizures at home.
<u>Stroke</u>	Sudden: numbness or weakness of face, arm, or leg difficulty speaking or understanding trouble seeing trouble walking dizziness or balance loss severe headache	*Minutes matter* – in the case of a stroke. The sooner your person gets medical attention, the better the outcome. Keep your person comfortable and resting until help comes.

Emergency	Warning signs / symptoms	Tips – *before help arrives*
Medication: Overdoses or Adverse Reactions	confusion, diminished mental status, or unusual forgetfulness nausea and vomiting faintness, dizzy, fatigue cold / clammy skin breathing difficulties	Determine if possible medication involved and save bottles to show to paramedics. Do not give your person anything to eat or drink. Observe breathing and pulse. **Refer to your CPR training card.** Begin rescue breathing or CPR if needed.
Falls and Broken Bones	Swelling, bruising, or bleeding Intense pain Out-of-place or deformed limb or joint Limited mobility or inability to move limb	If your person is on the floor and has pain. *Do not move them.* Make them comfortable. The paramedics can move them. If there are signs of a sprain or broken bone after a fall. Make them comfortable in chair or bed – immobilize, elevate, and apply ice to the injured area.
Burns	Red, painful, blisters Grey, white, pale, open burn	**Refer to your first aid training card.** Ask the 9-1-1 operator for what to do for your person's burn before help arrives. Do not attempt to clean or wrap burns. Keep your person lying quiet and calm.
Bleeding	Extremity cuts or injury Head wounds (ears) Internal – coughing or vomiting up blood or *coffee ground* material Internal – passing blood in urine or stool; black *tar-like* bowel movements.	**Refer to your first aid training card.** To control external bleeding: Apply direct pressure over the area of the wound with a clean cloth or sterile gauze pad. Apply firm, steady pressure 5-15 minutes. Elevate injured foot, leg, hand, or arm above level of your person's heart. For internal bleed, have your person lie flat.

Accident Prevention

Remember the saying – "an ounce of prevention is worth a pound of cure". You as a caregiver can prevent accidents by <u>practicing safety.</u> Focus on the task at hand. Do one task at a time. Be observant.

You can prevent a burn/scalding by checking the shower water before your person gets wet. You can prevent a fire by turning off the stove burner if the phone rings while you are cooking. You can prevent a fall by keeping the floors clear of clutter or walking with your person when there is not a handrail.

> *Practice keeping the home environment safe.*

Preventing a burn, a fire, or a fall might save your person from an emergency room visit, a hospital stay or save their life. Your person can prevent accidents with their own actions. They can slow down, focus on one task, and sit down if they feel tired or dizzy.

Falls and Fractures

Among older adults, falls are a serious health problem. A fall can result in a bone fracture. If your person has osteoporosis a fall can result in a hip fracture. A serious injury from a fall can limit your person from remaining active and living independently.

<u>**Personal Factors**</u> Personal factors which cause falls include muscle weakness, balance problems, slower reflexes, changes in vision or hearing, infections, and taking medications that may cause dizziness, fatigue, or confusion. Psychological factors include the fear of falling, depression, or a denial of a problem.

<u>**Environmental Factors**</u> Environmental factors include hazards in the home such as spills on floors, clutter, loose rugs, and stairs without handrails, poor lighting, and bathtubs without grab bars or skid-resistant mats. Hazards out side the home include uneven sidewalks, ice or snow, steps without railings, poor lighting in parking lots, and spills on grocery store floors.

Fall Prevention   Take these steps to prevent falling:

- Practice some form of daily exercises to maintain or improve body strength, flexibility, and balance.

- Stay hydrated – drink water. Limit alcohol usage which impairs balance and slows reflexes.

- Eat to keep strong bones – drink low fat milk or other products to meet your body's calcium needs.

- Have your person's vision and hearing checked and corrected – often.

- Watch your person for signs of illness or infection;   side effects, adverse reactions and medication interactions. Have a doctor review all medications that may increase the risk of falling.

- Have your person always sit for a moment before getting out of bed – stand up slowly from sitting – pause to find their balance before taking that first step.

- Encourage independence – have your person use a cane, walker, scooter or handrails – using caution when walking – paying attention to where they step.

- Wear nonskid, flat sole shoes with laces that support feet. Check feet for sores or long toenails.

- Immediately clean up spills, keep the walkways clutter free, and turn on lights before entering rooms.

- Review room safety checklists in Chapter 6 for other home safety ideas.

- Keep a cordless phone by your chair – to avoid *jumping up* to answer the phone.

- Be *extra cautious* when walking outside the house and in public places.

- Use a grocery cart for balance and to carry grocery bags to the car.

Consult with your doctor – anytime your person falls.

Medication Services

> This chapter addresses the importance of your person and the medication they take. Learn about their medication. Creating medication records -- keeping a current list of all medication and logging when medications are taken - helps avoid medication errors. Medication organizers are introduced. Finally, how the medication enters your person's body or *medication routes* are presented.

Medication is used to maintain health or to prevent or treat an illness, injury, or disease. In this book the word *medication* includes any prescription medication, non-prescription drug, or dietary supplements. If you have any questions about any medications you should consult with your doctor, pharmacist, or nurse.

A *prescription* medication is one that requires a prescription from a doctor for the pharmacy to sell you the medication. Examples of these medications are Lasix or Furosemide (a diuretic), Synthroid or Levorthyoxine (a thyroid hormone), or Verapamil or Calan (treats hypertension).

A non-prescription drug or *over-the-counter (OTC)* drugs can be purchased without a doctor's written order. Examples of these medications are Robitussin (cold or flu), aspirin or Tylenol (pain), or Benadryl (allergy).

Dietary supplements include vitamins, minerals, or herbal therapies.

Tell your doctor, if you take over-the-counter drugs or dietary supplements. Your doctor can discuss with you the drug interactions between these medications.

A label on the prescription bottle contains the following information:

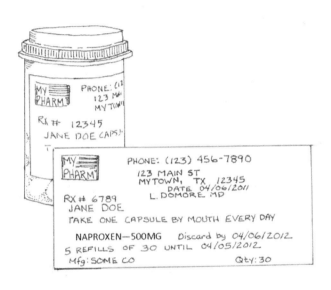

Patient's name
Doctor's name
pharmacy name, address, and
    telephone number
prescription number
date filled by pharmacy
medication name (if generic,
    also the brand name)
strength of the medication
quantity in the bottle
number of refills
date the medication expires
dosage
frequency
route information

The pharmacy supplies a printed patient information sheet with each medication called a monograph. The label data is repeated, but additional detailed information about taking the medication is listed. Reading the monograph covers topics such as common uses, how to use this medication, cautions, and possible side effects.

Over the counter drug and dietary supplement labels also include the product name, product strength, "Drug Facts" or "Supplement Facts". The information on the label, box, or additional information sheet might include directions, suggested uses, warnings, and other helpful information. Each product should also have an expiration date printed on the bottle or box.

You can purchase and keep a current (copyright within 2 years) copy of a drug reference guide in your medication area. These books such as *The Pill Book*, *Saunders Nursing Drug Handbook*, or *PDR Pocket Guide to Prescription Drugs* are sources of comprehensive drug information.

> ***If you have any questions about the medication, check with your doctor, pharmacist, or nurse.***
>
> ***Do not share prescription medication with another person.***

Storing medications

Store all medication in a dry and safe place. If practical, store medication in the bathroom medicine cabinet or a handy kitchen cabinet. Medications can be stored together in a movable container such as a plastic box or small basket. Some medications require refrigeration. Always store the medications in their original containers. Lock medications in a cabinet if there are children or confused people in the home.

Side Effects, Adverse Reactions, and Medication Interactions

To avoid potential problems with medications the person, caregiver, or family needs to be aware and observant of what medications the person is taking and how it is making the person feel.

Side effects are unplanned symptoms or feelings a person has when taking medication. For example, having a dry mouth or feeling drowsy. Most side effects are not serious and disappear on their own.

Adverse reactions are harmful or unfavorable side effects, such as severe or continuous diarrhea. Other adverse reactions might be a diminished mental status, confusion, or unusual forgetfulness.

Using alcohol and certain medications can cause severe adverse reactions.

Medication interactions is when one medication interacts with other medications, food or beverages, or your body's medical conditions.

A medication to medication interaction is where one medication increases or decreases the effectiveness of another medication. For example, taking both anxiety and allergy medications can slow your body reactions.

Certain foods can interfere with medication absorption – like grapefruit. Beverages with caffeine can interact with medications. It is best to take most medications with a glass of water. Tell your doctor how much alcohol you drink, before you begin any medication.

Existing medical conditions make certain medications potentially harmful. For example, if you have high blood pressure or asthma, there might be an unwanted reaction if a nasal decongestant is used for a cold.

> *Consult your doctor, if your person experiences any unwanted side effect, adverse reaction, or interaction.*
>
> *Avoid medication errors -- know each medication taken, track taking medication, and use a medication organizer*

Medication Records

It can be helpful to keep written medication records. Keep a separate medication record for each person. Do not combine records for two different people. The medication record can be as simple or complex as needed. Be sure to keep completed records with the care plan as they can be helpful data at doctor appointments.

Current Medication Chart

A current Medication Chart is useful to you to understand at a glance everything about the medication your person is taking. You create the medication chart by gathering all current medications and use the label to fill in the columns. Included information:

- Person's name

- Name of medication, dosage, amount, and frequency

- What it is taken for and a description of what it looks like

- Doctor who prescribed it

- Date it was started (date of doctor's order)

- When to take it (*e.g. on an Empty Stomach, with Meals, Bedtime*, PRN)

- Special instructions (e.g. keep refrigerated)

Sample **Current Medication Chart**

Name:			Date last updated:		Completed by:
#	Medication	Dose	Amount, Frequency	Looks like	Comments
1	Synthroid	100mcg	1 pill, Once a day	Small pill, round, yellow	For thyroid, take on empty stomach in am. Dr. White (PCP)
2	Naproxen	220mg	2 caplets, two times a day	Caplet, Oval, light blue	Anti-inflammatory for pain, take with food 12 hours apart. Dr. White
3	Restasis	Drop	Twice a day	Eye drops	For dry eye, instill in right eye and then left eye in morning and again before bed. Keep eyes closed for one minute. Dr. Black (eyes)
Know allergies:			Sulfa, penicillin, and bee stings		

See Chapter 5, Care Plan for a blank medication chart to copy/use.

Medication Log Sheet

> *A medication log sheet lists medications, the time of day they are to be taken, and columns that are filled in when the medication is actually taken.*

If your person is living alone and takes medication, this log sheet helps them keep track of when they took their medication. Or a medication log sheet can be used by the caregiver(s) who monitors or provides the daily medication.

It is important to be aware of the schedule and medication needs. If you are keeping your own record or only one family member is giving the medication, initials are not needed. Check marks can indicate the medication as taken.

Basic Medication Log Sheet

Name:			Month/Year				
Medication Dose Route Frequency	Date Time Initials **Mon.**	Date Time Initials **Tues.**	Date Time Initials **Weds.**	Date Time Initials **Thurs.**	Date Time Initials **Fri.**	Date Time Initials **Sat.**	Date Time Initials **Sun.**
Synthroid 100mcg 1 tablet; By mouth ½ hour before breakfast	6/8 7:30 am cc	6/9 7:30 am Ann	6/8 7:30 am cc				
Restasis 1 drop into both eyes Twice daily approx. 12 hours apart	7:30 am cc 7:30 pm cc	am Ann pm Ann	7:30 am cc				
Naproxen 220mg 2 tablets; by mouth Twice daily with food	8:30 am cc 8:30 pm-cc	am Ann pm Ann	8:30 am-cc				

Blank weekly and monthly logs can be found on the next pages for you to copy and use.

If your person has complex medication needs, for example takes several medications, some more than once a day and also is taking a short term medication, such as an antibiotic, then a medication log can be very valuable to insure correct medication administration is given. You can also use this complex format using monthly columns.

A blank complex log can be found on the next pages for you to copy and use.

Creating a Medication Log Sheet: To create the log sheet, refer to the *Medication Chart* to complete the first column. To save time, copy several (empty) hand written records with just the medication data completed. Mark the extra copies for future weeks or months. At the end of each month, review the new copy and make correction if needed.

Terminology Shortcuts

The chart below lists helpful common medication terminology shortcuts:

bid (*2 times a day*)	tid (*3 times a day*)	qid (*4 times a day*)
ac (*before meals*)	pc (*after meals*)	hs (*bedtime*)
qd (*every day*)	qod (*every other day*)	PRN (*medication given as needed*)
q4h (*every 4 hours*)	q6h (*every 6 hours*)	

Weekly Medication Log Sheet

Name:					Month/Year		
Medication **Dose** **Route** **Frequency**	Date Time Initials **Mon**.	Date Time Initials **Tues**.	Date Time Initials **Weds**.	Date Time Initials **Thurs**.	Date Time Initials **Fri**.	Date Time Initials **Sat.**	Date Time Initials **Sun.**

Monthly Medication Log Sheet

Name:

Month/Year

Medication Dose Route Frequency	1	2	3	4	5	6	7	8	9	10	11	12	13	14	15	16	17	18	19	20	21	22	23	24	25	26	27	28	29	30	31

Complex Medication Log Sheet

Name:		Month/Year					
Medication **Dose** **Route** **Frequency**	Date Time Initials **Mon.**	Date Time Initials **Tues.**	Date Time Initials **Weds.**	Date Time Initials **Thurs.**	Date Time Initials **Fri.**	Date Time Initials **Sat.**	Date Time Initials **Sun.**
Before breakfast							
With breakfast							
With lunch							
With dinner							
Before bedtime							

Medication Organizers

You can purchase medication organizers at stores that sell over-the-counter medications. They can hold a complete week's worth of medication. They are plastic containers that are designed to hold doses of medication and are divided according to date or time increment.

There are two basic sizes. One has seven compartments and has the day's initial on the lid. The other has 28 compartments with the day and time on the lid.

Medication organizers must be filled and used with extreme caution

<u>Filling a Medication Organizer</u>: To fill an organizer with a week's worth of medication, start by placing the current written *Medication Chart*, the actual medication bottles, and the organizer on a clean, dry table or counter. Be sure there is good lighting, which will enable you to see the colors of each pill. Allow time to complete this task without any interruptions.

Working with only ONE medication at a time, work your way down the *Medication Chart*. Carefully fill the medication organizer with the correct number of pills for each compartment of the organizer. Keep the medication bottles – even if they are empty.

Continue with this process until you have completed all the medications on the *Medication Chart*. Return the medication bottles to their storage location.

If you have concerns, ask your pharmacist, nurse, or family member to help you set up the medication organizer the first time.

Medication organizers should be handled just like the medication bottles. Keep them in a safe, dry location. Keep them in a locked location – if there are children or confused persons in the home.

Refills, expired medication, and discontinued medication

If your person takes medication on a continuing basis, it is up to you to ensure a constant supply is always available. Using a calendar is one method of tracking when refills are needed. You can also check the bottles of all medications every Sunday afternoon, looking for at least one week's supple of every medication. If you are filling medication organizers, you can track the need for refills at that time. If you do not have enough medication to complete a seven day period, then be sure to add calling the pharmacy to your task-list.

Look on the label of any medication for an expiration date. Follow the label or patient information directions, if any, for disposal of expired medications. Do not flush medications down the toilet unless this information specifically instructs you to do so.

If there are no instructions provided, the Food and Drug Administration (FDA) recommends that you throw the drugs in the household trash. But first – take the medications out of their original containers and mix them with an undesirable substance like coffee grounds or kitty litter. Put the mixture in a sealed bag, empty can or other container to prevent the medication from leaking or breaking out of a garbage bag.

If the medication is discontinued you should discard it as discussed above.

Infrequently used medication, such as seasonal cough syrup, should be stored in a safe and dry location. Before using check the expiration date and discard if expired.

Medication Routes

The table below shows various ways medication can be administered into a person's body. Always wash your hands before you handle medications. Review the label instructions with medication that is not given orally.

Before offering medication – DOUBLE CHECK – Right medication – Right time – Right dose – Right route

Route	Examples	Tips
Oral (mouth)	tablet or chewable tablet gel-cap capsule timed-released capsule liquids (syrup or elixir) sublingual tablet lozenges	Start with offering a drink of water. Then have the person take medication, one at a time with water or liquid. If giving sublingual medication, place it under the tongue or in cheek until it is completely dissolved. Do not swallow or chew the tablet.
Topical (skin)	trans-dermal (patch) creams or ointments spray or powder medication lotions	For skin applications, wash the affected area and pat dry. If using patches, make sure the old patch is off before applying a new one. Apply the patch to a clean and hair free area and alternate placement locations on body.
Installation	nasal spray eye drops	Have person in a sitting position. Put pump nozzle in clean nostril and use as directed on label. For eyes, soak any crusty areas of the eyes with a warm moist wash cloth for several minutes. Take special care to keep the dropper sterile, by not actually touching the eye. Have the person keep their eye shut for 15-30 seconds after putting in a drop.

Route	Examples	Tips
<u>Installation</u>	ear drops	For ear drops, have the person lay on their side. Cleanse the outer ear with a moist warm wash cloth if there is drainage. Have the person remain on their side for a few minutes to retain the medication in the ear.
	vaginal cream or suppositories	For vaginal care, ask the woman lay on her back with her knees slightly bent. Cleanse area if needed. Apply cream as directed or insert a lubricated suppository.
	rectal suppository	For rectal suppositories, ask the person to lay on their left side with their right leg drawn up towards the body. Cleanse area if needed. Lubricate the suppository and gloved finger. Ask the person to relax and take a deep breath. Spread the buttocks to expose the anus and gently insert the suppository about 4 inches into the rectum. Ask the person to remain on their side for 5 minutes and try to reframe from passing stool for the next hour.
<u>Inhalation</u> <u>(spray or mist)</u>	metered dose inhaler nebulizer	Ask your doctor or nurse to train you.
<u>Parenteral</u> <u>(needle)</u>	intramuscular (IM) intravenous (IV) subcutaneous (sq)	Ask your doctor or nurse to train you when required to use medications by injection.

When applying creams or suppositories, after washing hands, use gloves if recommended or desired.

Care Plan and Medical Records

A care plan is a collection of written information about your person's medical care needs. A care plan – like life itself – is an ever changing set of documents. Date each document when you finish. Initial and date any updates as they are added. Like a road map, it shows where you have been and where you are going.

A care plan includes an initial medical history, functional and medication services assessments, specific care to be provided and by whom. Medication records, treatment plans, and tracking sheets for vital signs, skin assessments, and/or blood sugar readings are also a part of the care plan. If you have hired a home health agency or a hospice agency, keep the paperwork they provide with the care plan.

The *Emergency – Paramedic Sheet* and the *Contact Information Sheet* are kept with the care plan to be immediately available when there is an urgent need.

Medical records compliment the care plan. They can include separate sections for each type of medical professional your person needs – primary care physician, any specialists (such as rheumatologist or cardiologist), vision specialist, hearing aid provider, or dentist. Other sections include lab results, x-ray reports, other medical test results, and a record of shots within past 3-5 years.

Organizing Paperwork: Start with a 2-inch three-ring binder or 12 pocket plastic accordion folder.. Create sections about each topic covered in this chapter. Keep it in a handy place for convenient and immediate reference.

> *Purchase multi-colored opaque binder pockets to help you organize your binder.*

Label the tabs of your binder or accordion folder with the following sections. Place folders or face sheets to identify the subsections.

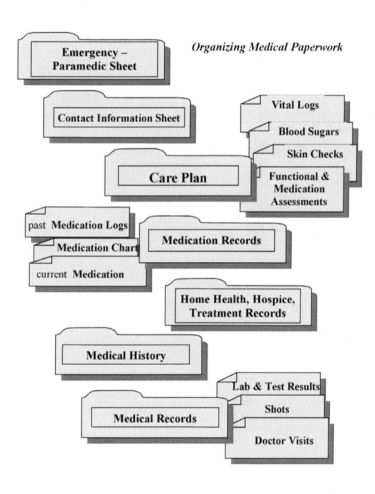

Organizing Medical Paperwork

- Emergency – Paramedic Sheet
- Contact Information Sheet
- Care Plan
  - Vital Logs
  - Blood Sugars
  - Skin Checks
  - Functional & Medication Assessments
- Medication Records
  - past Medication Logs
  - Medication Chart
  - current Medication
- Home Health, Hospice, Treatment Records
- Medical History
- Medical Records
  - Lab & Test Results
  - Shots
  - Doctor Visits

Medical History

Creating a medical history.. helps you understand more about your person and documents a written record. Spend the time to ask your person questions about their past and present medical conditions. As you create the history, encourage your person to share their memories and feelings. Take this completed page(s) with you when you see a new doctor.

Below are some example questions. Add additional information to the history as you need.

- Are your parents living? Age and cause of death? Brothers or sisters. Aunts or uncles.

- What health diagnosis did your mother, father, brother, or sister have?
    Make a list with names.

- How many children? Living? Ages? Health diagnosis?

- Habits – Did/do you smoke? How many packs a day for how many years?

- Habits – Did/do you drink alcoholic beverages? How many per day or week?

- Lifestyle – How active are you?
    Do you exercise? Type of exercise and how much or how often?

- Do you wear glasses?   Partial or complete dentures?   Hearing aids?

- What surgeries have you had?   Dates?

- Hospitalizations? Dates?

- What are previous health diagnoses
    – like a past bleeding ulcer or pneumonia 3 years ago?

- If you have had cancer – list type and dates of last radiation or chemo.

- What are your current health diagnoses?
    Create a list – include onset date and treatment history.
    Include as much detail in this section as possible.

- Do you have any allergies to medications – list adverse reactions?

- Date of last physical exam. Date of last blood work or laboratory tests.
    Date of last x-rays.

Diagnosis Guidelines: Research and gather basic information about each diagnosis your person has. Place this folder of information in the *Medical History* section for quick reference and explanations.

Functional Assessment

Functional skills are discussed in *Supervisory Care* and *Personal Care*. They are based on your person's physical and psychosocial health. This assessment should document any reason why your person needs caregiving. Add specific text about the type of care, the level of care, and goals of care for each topic. If others provide the care, indicate who gives the care, such as which family member, a paid caregiver, hospice/home health nurse, or physical therapist.

Start with an initial assessment including medication services. Review the assessment every 3-6 months or whenever your person has a change of caregiving needs. Keep the most current functional assessment handy to share with any other caregivers or to take with you to doctor visits.

Supervisory Care Assessment

.Example topics for *Supervisory Care*:

- Is your person able to drive?
- Is your person partially or completely blind or deaf?
- Is your person depressed, lonely, isolated from others, or frail?
- Is your person able to cook a meal or able to heat up leftovers?
- Does your person require a special diet?
- Does your person need an advocate at a doctor's appointment?
- Is your person able to get help from you or others if they fall or are sick?

<u>NOTES:</u>

Sample of a *partial* **Supervisory Care Functional Assessment and Care Plan**

Irene has glaucoma. She is able to see well enough to still live independently in her senior apartment. The goal is to keep Irene contently and safely living alone.

1. Irene likes help with house cleaning. Her daughter Lynn has hired a house cleaner to come once a week. Irene is able to direct this person.

2. Irene is not able to drive. Lynn or church members are able to drive Irene anytime she needs a ride.

3. Irene is a very social person. She likes to visit with her friends at the recreation center. She also likes to exercise in the pool. A neighbor has volunteered to walk with and stay with Irene at the pool or recreation center in the mornings during the week.

4. Irene has asked Lynn to be with her at all doctor appointments. Lynn schedules the appointment, discusses and documents her questions before they go. Lynn drives her to the doctor, goes into the examining room with her, and writes down the answers and directions from the doctor.

5. Irene has a large button phone. The speed-dial is programmed for Lynn's cell phone, her next door neighbor and for 9-1-1. If Irene needs urgent care, she is able to yell or call on the phone for help.

Written by:_____   Dated: _____

Notes/Updates:

Personal Care Assessment

.Example questions for *Personal Care*

- What activities of daily living require my attention? Grooming, dressing, bathing?
- Is your person incontinent? Bladder? Bowel?
- Is your person able to walk alone, with a cane, with a walker, or with my assistance?
- Does your person use a wheelchair inside the house?
- Does your person need your help with transfers between a bed and chair?
- Is your person non-ambulatory?
- Does your person need help with monitoring and recording their vital signs?
- Does your person have a skin rash or pressure sore?

<u>NOTES:</u>

Sample of a *partial* **Personal Care Functional Assessment and Care Plan**

Lucy Mae has had a stroke. She spent 2 weeks at a rehabilitation care center and is now back living in her own home with her son Donald. Her left arm is partially paralyzed from the shoulder to her finger tips. Her entire left side is weak.

1. Lucy Mae needs Donald to help her move between her bed, wheelchair, toilet, and the dining room chairs. The physical therapist at the care center taught Donald how to stand on Lucy Mae's strong side and help her slowly and safely change her location.

2. Lucy Mae is continent, but she needs Donald's assistance on/off the toilet. For privacy, Donald attached a jingle bell on the door knob. She jingles it when she wants him to return to the bathroom.

3. Lucy May is receiving 1 hour of physical therapy, three days a week. A physical therapist comes to the house.

4. Lucy Mae needs help with bathing and washing her hair. Donald has a paid caregiver from the home health agency to help Lucy Mae with these tasks 3 days each week.

Written by:_____   Dated: _____

Notes/Updates:

Medication Services Assessment

.Example topics for *Medication Assistance*

- Does your person understand each and every medication they take and why they take it? What medications do they take?
- Is your person able to independently take their medication properly?
- Does your person require assistance in obtaining, storing, or taking their medication?
- Does your person require you to set-up a weekly medication organizer?

Current Medication Chart

Name:			Date last updated:		Completed by:	
#	Medication	Dose	Frequency	Looks like	Comments	
1						
2						
3						
4						
5						
Know allergies:						

Sample of a *partial* **Medication Functional Assessment and Care Plan**

Harold has Parkinson's disease. Harold understands the takes medication for his illness.

1. Harold knows he is to take 2 (color) tablets (name) with breakfast and 1 (color) tablet (name) with dinner.

2. He also knows he takes a red and white (Tylenol, 500mg) capsule before bedtime.

3. His wife helps him obtain these medications from the pharmacy. She has purchased a plastic medication organizer that has four daily compartments for each day of the week.

4. On Mondays she fills the compartments with the correct medications.

5. Harold keeps this medication organizer on the kitchen table. He remembers to take his pills according to the directions on the bottles, which are stored in the kitchen   cabi-net.

Written by:_____   Dated: _____

Notes/Updates:

NOTES:

Memory Care Assessment

.In addition to supervisory and personal care – this assessment and care plan also documents specifically the memory, thinking, judgment, or other mental impairments of your person.

Example questions for Memory Loss Care

- How is your person's memory impaired?
- How is your person's judgment or thinking impaired?
- What is your person's mental diagnosis and what does that involve?
- Does your person have a *Life Story*?
- What supervisory or personal care tasks are needed?
  (such as help with transportation or Activities of Daily Living)
- What medication services are needed?
- What behaviors does your person have? (See *Memory Care-Behaviors*)
- Does your person require Palliative Care?

NOTES:

Sample of a *partial* **Memory Loss Care Functional Assessment and Care Plan**

Grant has Alzheimer's disease. He is 85 years old. He was diagnosed with signs of dementia 5 years ago. Grant lives at home with his wife, Maria who is his representative and caregiver.

1. Grant has short term memory loss. He does not like to be left alone. He easily tires. His ability to do complex and familiar tasks is declining. He frequently repeats a question.

2. Grant is able to do all activities of daily living – with reminders and coaching.

3. Grant is continent. He requires reminders to use the bathroom before leaving home.

4. Grant is taking medication for high cholesterol. Maria places the medication and daily vitamins in a small cup and observes Grant take the pills with his breakfast.

5. Grant has spent much of his life being outdoors. He enjoys short (15 minute) walks in good weather and is willing to help with yard work.

6. Grant enjoys and goes to an Adult Day Health Care center on Mon./Wed./Friday. The center van stops at the house at 8:25 am and returns Grant to the house at 3:10 pm.

7. Grant shadows (follows) Maria and other visitors – if they leave the room. He enjoys finger snacks, showing pictures of his children from his wallet, and drying the dishes.

8. Grant enjoys watching golf, football games, and the nightly news on the TV.

9. Grant and Maria go to church on Sunday. They enjoy spending time with church friends.

Written by:_____ Dated: _____

Notes/Updates:

*(This assessment includes **all** the cognitive or mental health, supervisory and personal care, and medication services needed to meet the needs of the person with memory loss.)*

Medication Records Documenting the medication your person takes is discussed in *Medication Services* (Chapter 4).

.Medication records include a current medication chart and a daily medication log. This section of the care plan is where you keep current and past medication records.

Vital Logs Taking and/or measuring vital signs. such as body temperature, respiration, pulse, blood pressure and weight are discussed in *Personal Care*. Determine a tracking sheet format that is best for your use. If you infrequently document this information, you can log the date of the measurement and write in the numbers. Leave a line or space between dates.

Use a separate sheet with columns and headings, if for example you are tracking on a more frequent basis your person's blood pressure every Sunday and Thursday in the morning and before bed time. This allows you to compare differences. You can take these logs with you to a doctor's visit.

Another example of frequent measurements is daily monitoring of blood sugar, as discussed in *Personal Care*.

Skin Assessments If your person has any skin rash, red area, cuts, bruises, or other skin breakdown, document what you see. Note when you called the doctor or nurse. Include any instructions you receive about providing care for this finding. Keep routine notes until the skin is completely healed.

Home Health Agencies

Home Health agencies. can be an enormous benefit to a solo-caregiver. If you hire external help, the agency has their set of paperwork requirements. You can expect an initial assessment and written agreement of exactly what service(s) they are providing and costs involved.

Every time an agency staff member comes to your person's house, they should leave a copy of their paperwork for that day. This paper gives the date and name of staff member. It also lists what specific tasks they did – such as Judy W. came to the house on Monday, (date) from 8:30-9:30 am. She helped Wanda with a shower, washed and dried her hair, and did a skin check. No skin breakdown was seen. Judy will be back this week on Wednesday and Friday to help Wanda with her shower.

After a hospital visit, home health agencies often provide continued medication administration, medical assessments/monitoring, or physical therapy treatments. In this case, there are written doctor's orders to the agency that indicate what service(s) they are providing. This allows your person to continue to recover in their own home setting and avoiding an extended recovery period in a rehab or nursing care facility.

Treatment Records

If you have a physical therapist, a wound care nurse, or other health care professional providing specific treatment in the home, then keep copies of the treatment records.

Hospice Agencies

.If your person is under Hospice care (see *Palliative Care*), the Hospice agency will furnish you with a copy of their initial assessment, the hospice care plan, and hospice medication records. Every time a hospice staff member comes to the house – they should leave a copy of their paperwork for that day.

Emergency – Paramedic Sheet

.This simple sheet is intended to be ***handed to a paramedic or emergency room staff*** when your person has an accident, acute illness, or other life-threatening incident. Provide information for the following four areas. Make a second copy that remains in the care plan for your information.

<u>Identification</u> List the person's full name, address, and age, date of birth, and social security (or Medicare) number.

<u>Diagnosis and Medical Conditions</u> Provide as much information as possible in short, specific sentences. List all known diagnosis and medical conditions. Indicate if your person cannot hear, see, or does not speak or understand English. Indicate and attach copies of any health care directives.

<u>Emergency Contact Information</u> Provide name of individual(s) to be contacted incase of emergency (spouse, children, or other), phone numbers, and addresses. List name and phone numbers of primary doctor or specialists. List name and phone number of Hospice agency.

<u>Current Medication Chart</u> Attach a copy of your person's current medication chart. See *Medication Services.*

Contact Information Sheet

These sheets are used by the caregiver or your person like a phone and address book. One sheet should contain emergency contact information. Other sheets contain names of all contacts applicable to the care of the person such as family, friends, doctors, pharmacy, church, pastor, transportation services, hospital, ambulance, funeral home, etc.

Emergency—Paramedic Sheet

Name:

Address:

Social Security/Medicare number:

Date of Birth   Current age

Diagnosis and Medical Conditions:

Please contact these people in case of an emergency:

☐ **Attached are copies of my Advance Directives.**

☐ **Attached is a copy of my current chart of medication taken.**

Highlight frequently used phone numbers for quick reference.

List the person's name and phone numbers (home, cell, work, and fax). Include other helpful information such as addresses, web-pages, e-mail addresses, or business name.

Medical Records

This section can be helpful for both the person receiving care and the caregiver living with the person. The practice of keeping personal medical records is valuable for one's own health. Keep a separate notebook or accordion folder for yourself. When they get thick – file the prior year(s) separately.

Medical Appointments Typically you will make an appointment with a particular doctor to a specific reason. Depending upon your person's need create a pre-appointment cheat sheet. Indicate what information needs to be told to the doctor. Write down any questions – leaving space to write down the answers. When you are at the doctor's office, also write down any additional instructions you receive. File this sheet behind the tab with the doctor's name.

Lab Results, X-ray Reports, Test Results At every doctor visit, request copies of all lab results, x-ray reports, and other test results. As an informed person, you can share information with other family members or other doctors to the benefit of your person or yourself.

Be sure to have your person tested for TB (tuberculosis) every year.

Shot record If you see more than one doctor, it is important to keep a record of what shot was given on what date. Some shots are annual, like the flu shot. Other shots are not given annually, like the shingles shot, pneumonia shot, and tetanus shot.

The Paper Chase

This chapter addresses locating, creating, completing and organizing financial, legal, advance directives, and other important documents. These documents include financial (car title, life or medical insurance, investments), estate planning (wills, codicils, trusts), advanced directives (living will, medical and mental health care powers of attorney) and funeral directives (mortuary plan or pre-paid contract, obituary, or service).

Refer to Care Plans and Medical Records to create a care plan, contact information sheets, and organize medical records.

Neat paper work and good planning is essential throughout life's journey and *especially in times of crisis or change* — sudden injury, severe illness or when your person dies. Good planning relieves undue stress on the family, allows your person's personal wished to be honored, and communicates their values. It is critical to have these documents ready when they needed.

Always promote your person's dignity, independence, self-determination, privacy, and choice.

After skimming this chapter, start with a list of documents that you determine are essential. Consider purchasing a small locking medal filing cabinet. Set up folders for all the categories and create labels that are meaningful. File documents you have and determine steps to obtain, create, or complete others on your list. Some documents might need to be copied for the file and placed in a safe-deposit box at the bank.

Place a paper shredder in a handy location.

Communication Before you jump into action – take the time to discuss the following topics with your person. Depending upon the reason you are reading this book and this chapter – you might or *might not* know your persons needs and wishes. Respecting privacy and choice – determine your person's needs and wishes.

> *Be your person's advocate for their rights, needs, and wishes when communicating with others.*

Encourage them to talk to you, family members, or other people (loved ones, doctors, religious leaders, etc) about their wishes. It is important for your person to share their needs, decisions, and actions with appropriate the people. That way – down the road – these people will know what to expect and can follow the wishes of your person – bringing peace of mind and avoiding conflict.

Financial

For most, financial matters are personal and private topics. You can help your person with any paper work tasks – without actually seeing what the papers say. Have your person file the papers and keep the key on their key-ring.

Financial documents
- Car title, house title, mortgage papers, property tax statements
- Medicare card, supplemental health insurance policies, long-term care plans
- Life insurance policies
- Bank or investment statements, annuities, Certificates of Deposit, EE bonds
- Social security papers, pensions, railroad or veteran's retirement benefits
- Reverse mortgages, real estate owned with others
- Prior years of income tax forms, current year tax folder of receipts
- Medical statements and insurance payments
- Listing/pictures of valuables
    – jewelry, coin collections, silver table settings, heirlooms

Perhaps the largest financial risk for your person is the future cost of their health care. Risks include their age, life expectancy, current health, and how they are able to pay for *expected and unexpected* future health care needs.

Understanding the terms:

Social Security is a federal retirement program which pays back a percentage of a person's lifetime earnings. . It was never intended to be a person's only source of income, but rather to supplement other savings, investments, pensions and insurance plans. For more information call 1-800-772-1213 or visit www.socialsecurity.gov .

Medicare is a federal health insurance program for people age 65 and older. The program helps cover the cost of health care, but it does not cover all medical expenses or the cost of most long-term care. Order the guide *Medicare and You* (Pub no. CMS-10050) to get more detailed information about what Medicare covers. To get a copy call 1-800-633-4227 or visit www.medicare.gov .

Supplemental health insurance policies called *Medigap* policies can be purchased to cover costs **not covered by Medicare**. Order the guide *Choosing a Medigap Policy: A guide to health insurance for people with Medicare* (Pub no. CMS-02110) – see above – for more information/ tips.

Medicaid is a state-run program the provides hospital and medical coverage for people with **very low income and little or no resources.** Each state has its own set of rules about who is eligible and what is covered under Medicaid. Medicare and Medicaid are two different programs – although some people qualify for both Medicare and Medicaid. For more information about Medicaid contact the Area Agency on Aging for the number or website in your state.

Long-term care insurance is a type of insurance specifically to cover the costs of long-term care services, most of which are not covered by Medicare. The cost of the insurance is based on the type and amount of services you choose to be covered and how old the person covered is when the insurance is purchased. Your person might not qualify for long-term care insurance if they are in poor health or already receiving long-term care services. The U.S. Department of Human and Health Services provides a website www.longtermcare.gov which gives information about *Coverage and Benefit Choices* and many more long-term care insurance topics.

Estate Planning

The organization of financial documents helps your person to understand their assets, belongings, income sources and amounts, and liabilities (what they owe on mortgage or other loans). Creating an estate plan enables your person to conserve or protect their assets and income, determine how their assets and income are spent to benefit their care while living, and pass on the remaining contents of their estate to their heirs.

Discuss with your person the importance of protecting their wealth. Consider a consultation with an attorney who specializes in elder law or estate planning. *One-size does not fit all* – and understanding what is best for your person requires help from someone who can explain to you and your person all the available options. An attorney can explain how specific laws vary state to state and make necessary updated to existing documents if the laws have changed or your elder has moved to a new state.

An estate plan may include a living trust and/or a will. A codicil can be mentioned in the will and attached as an amendment. The original documents need to be placed in a safe deposit box. Copies can be kept in a safe place or given to a trusted family member or trusted friend.

A **living trust** is a way of protecting assets from probate and perhaps from inheritance taxes. An attorney is needed initially to write the trust document. Your person's property belongs to the trust – which can be controlled and changed by your person. If your person becomes incapacitated, their designated trustee manages the trust assets to benefit your person's financial needs. If your person dies the designated trustee transfers the trust assets to the beneficiaries according to the terms of the trust. Since no court supervision is required it is quicker and less costly to transfer assets to the named beneficiaries.

A **will** usually goes through state probate. In a will your person – in a written document – indicates how their assets are distributed to the named beneficiaries. The will can also indicate specifically who gets nothing from the estate. An executor is named in the will. The executor manages the estate from the time of death until the assets are distributed.

If a person does not have a will when they die, each state has laws that dictate what happens to your person's assets and belongings. A personal representative is appointed by the probate court to administer the estate. Families and friends may have little if any input to this process after your person dies.

A codicil is an appendix to a will. It is mentioned in the will and is a list of certain belongings and to who gets these items. For example – your person might want her fine china to go to a grandson (John), her crystal stemware to a grandson (Jack), her wedding ring to go to her oldest granddaughter (Jill).

Beneficiaries can be specifically named with certain assets. Life insurance policies and investment accounts – usually include beneficiary names and contact information. Certificates of deposit can specify a *payable on death (POD)* designee on the face of the certificate. With a spouse's permission, 401k and IRA accounts can name someone other than the spouse as a beneficiary. Multiple beneficiaries can be named – such as Jack (50%) and Jill (50%).

Your person is still able to use the income or principle of these assets – leaving the beneficiary any remaining funds. Beneficiaries can be changed by your person – as long as they are competent and able to communicate their wishes.

Other Legal Documents

Along with a living trust, will, and/or codicil include keeping the original copies birth certificates, marriage certificates, divorce decrees, military service/discharge papers, spouse or parent's death certificates in a safe deposit box.

Advanced Directives

Advanced planning, through the use of powers of attorney (POA) and living wills can help your person retain their dignity and independence. All states have laws that allow a person to make these future healthcare decisions – now. These laws also allow a person to appoint someone to make healthcare decisions for them in the event they are incapacitated. These documents are exercised when your person is permanently or temporarily unable to communicate or make decisions as determined by a doctor or medical emergency.

Advanced directives provide protection and a mechanism to assist in decision making. They are a legal process of making your person's healthcare and medical wishes known. Check your state attorney general's office web pages to determine how you can obtain and create these forms and have them witnessed as required by law – without the expense of hiring an attorney.

> *Life care planning is for everyone –*
> *Caregiver – complete your own set of Advanced Directives.*

Encourage your person to discuss their wishes – openly – so that they can make well reasoned choices in advance. This will ease the stress on you their caregiver, their family and friends, and help doctors and loved ones carry out their wishes in the future.

A **living will** allows your person to choose which medical procedures and interventions can be performed. The living will creates a statement that is unique to their wishes – such as if they desire *some or all* of the following: comfort care, CPR, ventilation, artificially administered food and fluids.

The living will does not become effective – unless your person is unable to communicate their decisions. Typically, it can be changed at anytime – as long as your person can talk, write, or otherwise communicate their wishes. The living will is important because it provides guidance to family members and doctors as they are treating your person at the end of their life.

Understanding the terms:

Comfort care – an effort to protect or enhance quality of life without artificially prolonging life – most often pain management, oxygen, offering (but not forcing) food or fluids, keeping the person clean, holding person's hand, and using soothing words or music.

CPR is cardiopulmonary resuscitation – used when your person's heart stops.

Ventilation – artificial breathing – using a ventilator, oxygen is administered using a tube through nose, mouth, or tracheotomy (a hole in throat).

Artificially administered fluids or food – intravenous treatments or feeding tubes.

A **Durable Health Care Power of Attorney** allows your person to select a person they trust as their representative to make future health care decisions for them if they can not make those decisions themselves. In most cases, this person is a close family member. It goes hand-in-hand with the living will – which is attached to the Health Care POA.

The representative and your person should talk about your person's choices. It is the representative's obligation to follow and advocate the expressed wishes made in writing by your person. A **Letter to My Representative** can be used to provide additional information on the role and responsibilities to the representative, such as preferences for pain management, if a home setting is desired at death, which loved ones you want at your bedside or if you would like to receive a final blessing by a clergy.

A **Durable Financial Power of Attorney** allows your person to select a person as their representative to handle and make decisions about their finances. A Durable POA can go into effect as soon as it is signed (if written that way) or when your person becomes incapacitated as determined by a doctor. A Health Care POA can also be written to include the power of managing financial decisions.

A **Durable Mental Health Care Power of Attorney** is beyond a Health Care POA as it allows your person to appoint a person to make future mental health care decisions for them. A representative is authorized to have your person admitted to a mental health facility – with 24 hour supervision and intensive treatment. A representative under a Health Care POA can not do this. A Mental Health Care POA is intended for persons with a history of mental illness.

A **Pre-Hospital Medical Care Directive** also known as a **DNR (Do not resuscitate)** order is a specifically written form that directs which life-saving actions are to be taken to taken – when a person is at the end stage of a terminal illness or near death. This form would be used by emergency medical personnel such as paramedics or the staff at the hospital's emergency room or other hospital or hospice staff. The form is used when your person desires to let nature take its course – rather than have medical professionals perform extreme measures to save their lives. This form is filled out – after a consultation with a doctor or hospital staff, who must also sign the form. The form indicates which resuscitation measures to forgo, including CPR, defibrillation, assisted ventilation, intubation and/or advanced life-support medications.

> *Keep original advance directives in a safe place.*
>
> *Put a copy of advance directives with the "Paramedic – Emergency Sheet".*

To honor your person's advance directives – your person's representative, doctor, hospital, hospice agency, or nursing facility must be aware of the advance directives and be aware of what they say. The representative, primary doctor and the hospital upon admission should have a copy of the advance directives.

What happens without Advance Directives

If advance directives do not exist and your person is found to be unable to care for themselves every state has rules to have a court appoint a suitable guardian and/or conservator to protect a vulnerable adult from harm. Health care providers (doctors and nurses) in hospitals and nursing facilities will try to find a guardian or a surrogate who has the authority to make health care decisions for your person.

Understanding the terms:

Incapacitated person – a person is incapacitated when they are either unable to communicate their decisions based on their medical condition or are incompetent as determined by a doctor.

Surrogate – each state has a surrogate statue that determines priorities decision makers within the family unit and others (for instance spouse before adult child, adult child before partner or friend, if there are more than 2 or more siblings, etc). A surrogate is an adult decision maker for an incapacitated person who does not have a designated representative or legal guardian and needs major medical treatment in a hospital or nursing facility.

Guardianship – a court appoints a guardian for an incapacitated person to make decisions concerning their housing, medical care, meals, clothing and social activities.

Conservatorship – a court appoints a conservator for an incapacitated person if a person has and is not capable of managing money and/or property effectively.

Often *family members or friends* ask the court for the legal authority to act as a guardian or conservator. It is when no one is willing to take the responsibility that the court appoints a private, public, or Veteran's fiduciary, as appropriate.

Funeral or Memorial Planning

Preplanning their own funeral or celebration of life provides family and loved ones a clear picture of your person's final wishes. My grandmother lived to be 100 years old – but she and my grandfather had purchased their side-by-side mausoleum spaces 20 years prior to her death. They shared a comforting vision of their final resting place.

Start with these questions:

- Do you want your body buried in a casket?
- Do you want to be cremated?
- Do you want a rosary or a visitation time?
- Do you have a special dress or suit?
- Do you want a traditional funeral or a celebration of life – tell me your ideas
- What pictures do you want displayed
  – your wedding, in your military uniform, your 50th anniversary
- Do you want certain songs, have you asked someone to sing, do you want a musician?
- Are there certain readings you would like read – by whom?
- Have you chosen pallbearers? Do you want a military salute or flag presentations?
- Have you purchased a cemetery plot or mausoleum space?
- Have you purchased a headstone? What do you want engraved on your headstone?
- Do you want your ashes spread in a special place or way; or do you want your ashes placed in a cemetery vault?

Create a funeral/memorial folder with any information you gather from talking with your person. Add to this folder as more documents and information are obtained. Compile contact numbers for the desired organist, singers, musicians, readers, or pallbearers.

Death Certificate Information

Compile the following information about your person on a sheet of paper. The funeral home will need it in order to finalize the death certificate. A copy of a birth certificate usually contains parent's data.

first, middle, last name		maiden name, if applicable	
home address		social security number	

date of birth		gender		race		date of death		age	

occupation		highest level of education		Birth city, state	

marital status		spouse's entire name		

father's name		birth city		birth state	
mother's name		birth city		birth state	

If your person is a Veteran, then copy their service discharge papers for veteran data is also needed.

The Obituary

Try using an interview approach to *pre-write* an obituary. Start with a list of the names, correctly spelled of your person's siblings, children, grand-children, and/or great-grand-children. Note if any have died. Ask her what accomplishments she wants mentioned. Ask about any charities that she would wish to include for memorial donations. Write up this interview in a story (rather than obituary) style. Omit any sentences about death or date of death. Read it to your person, asking for any corrections or additions.

Funeral Expenses

The Federal Trade Commission (FTC) makes available on their website a free copy of *"Funerals: A Consumer Guide"*. This guide walks the reader through helpful funeral topics and questions. This guide helps your person and/or others understand more about how to control costs of a funeral.

The FTC enforces the *Funeral Rule* as presented below.

According to the Funeral Rule:

- you have the right to choose the funeral goods and services you want (with some exceptions).
- the funeral provider must state *this right* in writing on the general price list.
- if state or local law requires you to buy any particular item, the funeral provider must disclose it on the price list, with a reference to a specific law.
- the funeral provider may not refuse, or charge a fee, to handle a casket you bought elsewhere.
- a funeral provider that offers cremations must make alternate containers available.

Copied from: www.ftc.gov/bcp/edu/pubs/consumer/products/pro19.pdf

---

***Print and read a copy of this guide* by the FTC.
Keep it in the funeral/memorial folder**

Knowledgeable caregiving can reduce risk, decrease stress, and increase everyone's happiness. In a nut shell:

♦ Supervisory care is *hands-off* and Personal care is *hands-on* caregiving. Memory loss care and Palliative care are both forms of comfort caregiving.

♦ Base your actions on respect. Be kind and patient. Always promote your person's dignity, independence, self-determination, privacy, and choice.

♦ Wash your hands often. Practice safety: focus on the task at hand; slow down - do not rush; be observant. Take a First Aid class and a CPR class.

♦ Give yourself grace, keep your sense of humor, address your own stress, and *take time for yourself*. Hire a housekeeper. Enlist others to help you with caregiving - family, friends, volunteers, or paid workers. Investigate your local Senior Centers or Adult Day Health Care Centers.

♦ *Consult your person's doctor or nurse* when... you observe frequent diarrhea, constipation, or unusual urine results... unexplained or sudden changes in weight... if you observe a rapid or irregular heart beat, changes in blood pressure, disorientation, drowsiness, headaches, or nausea... if your person is in pain, sick, or has an infection... any time your person falls... you find skin break down... when your person has any medication side effect, adverse reaction, or interaction... *any time you have a question or concern about your person's medication or medical needs.*

♦ Create a helpful paper trail. Use a medication chart and care plan. Complete a current contact list and an Emergency - Paramedic sheet. Encourage your person (and yourself) to complete Advance Directives paperwork. Advocate and respect these directives.

Enjoy the special relationship between yourself and your person.

Laugh Love Live   Enjoy your journey!

Index

A

Abuse
   abuse, neglect and exploitation, 92
   prevention, 93
   reporting abusive situations, 95
Accidents, 130
Activities, 20
   advanced dementia, with, 80
   memory loss care, with, 61
   palliative care, with, 77
Activities of Daily Living, 29
   bathing, 36
   dressing, 30
   eating, 32
   grooming, 29
   memory loss care, with, 57
   mobility and transfer, 31
   toileting, 34
Adult Day Health Care Centers, 25
Advanced directives, 168, 171
   DNR, 170
   financial POA, 169
   health care POA, 169
   living will, 168
   mental health care POA, 170
AIDS, 52
Alzheimer's Disease (AD), 52
   Alzheimer's Association, contacting, 53
   progressive stages, 52
Assessment, care plans, 149
   medication assistance, 154
   memory care, 156
   personal care, 152
   skin care, 158
   supervisory care, 150

B

Bathing, 36
   bed bath guidelines, 75
Bed rails
   side rails, do not use, 49, 114
Behaviors, memory loss, 67
   managing difficult behaviors, 69

   possible causes, 67
Bleeding. *See* page 129
Breathing problems, 74
Burns. *See* page 129

C

Calcium, 8
Calendar
   activity or exersice, 25
   event, 24
   senior center or adult day health care center, 25
Call buttons or bells, 34, 35, 49, 115
Calling for help, 125
Calories, daily, 10
Carbohydrates, 6
Care plan, 146
   emergency - paramedic sheet, 160
   home health agencies, 159
   hospice agencies, 159
   medical history, 148
   medication records, 158
   medication services assessment, 154
   memory care assessment, 156
   organizing, 147
   personal care assessment, 152
   supervisory care assessment, 150
   vital logs, 158
Caregiver stress, 97
Chemicals, 115
Choking. *See* page 127
Combustible or flammable liquids, 115
Comfort care
   activities, and, 61
   memory loss care, and, 54
   pets, 82
   specified in living will, 168
   spiritual, 83
   surroundings, 81
Communication, 87
   advanced directives, 168
   finacial or legal wishes, 164
   funeral or memorial planning, 172
   health updates, 83
   life story & memory loss, 63